Ancient Pueblo Peoples
"Anasazi"

Sohrab ChamanAra

Copyright © 2010 by Sohrab ChamanAra.

ISBN: Softcover   978-1-4535-1021-6
        Ebook   978-1-4535-1022-3

All rights reserved. No part of this book may be reproduced or transmitted in any form or by any means, electronic or mechanical, including photocopying, recording, or by any information storage and retrieval system, without permission in writing from the copyright owner.

This book was printed in the United States of America.

To order additional copies of this book, contact:
Xlibris Corporation
1-888-795-4274
www.Xlibris.com
Orders@Xlibris.com
81271

Contents

Ancient Pueblo Peoples "Anasazi" 1
Puebloan peoples 20
Spanish Colonization 21
New Mexico Pueblos 32
Acoma Pueblo 33
Cochiti Pueblo 37
Isleta Pueblow 38
Jemez Pueblo 40
Laguna Pueblo 41
Nambé Pueblo 44
Ohkay Owingeh Pueblo 45
Picuris Pueblo 47
Pojoaque Pueblo 48
Sandia Pueblo 49
Kachina 56
San Felipe Pueblo 58
San Ildefonso Pueblo 58
Santa Ana Pueblo 60
Santa Clara Pueblo 60
Santo Domingo Pueblo 61
Taos Pueblo 61
Tesuque Pueblo 65
Zia Pueblo 66

Zuni Pueblo 67
Arizona 74
Texas 92
Colorado 92
Feast days 93
Acknowledgement 101

Dedication:

This book is dedicated to the memory of those peaceful and civilized Native-Americans who suffered and perished in their struggle to defend and preserve their traditions and way of life.

Ancient Pueblo Peoples
"Anasazi"

Cliff Palace, Mesa Verde National Park (cover of the book).

White House Ruins, Canyon de Chelly National Monument.

Ancient Pueblo People or **Ancestral Puebloans** were an ancient Native American culture centered on the present-day Four Corners area of the

United States, comprising southern Utah, northern Arizona, northwest New Mexico, and a lesser section of Colorado. The cultural group has often been referred to in archaeology as the **Anasazi**, although the term is not preferred by the modern Puebloan peoples. The word *Anasazi* is Navajo for "Ancient Ones" or "Ancient Enemy".

Archaeologists still debate when this distinct culture emerged, but the current consensus, based on terminology defined by the Pecos Classification, suggests their emergence around 1200 BC, during the archaeologically designated Basketmaker II Era. Beginning with the earliest explorations and excavations, researchers have believed that the Ancient Puebloans are ancestors of the modern Pueblo peoples. In general, modern Pueblo people claim these ancient people as their ancestors.

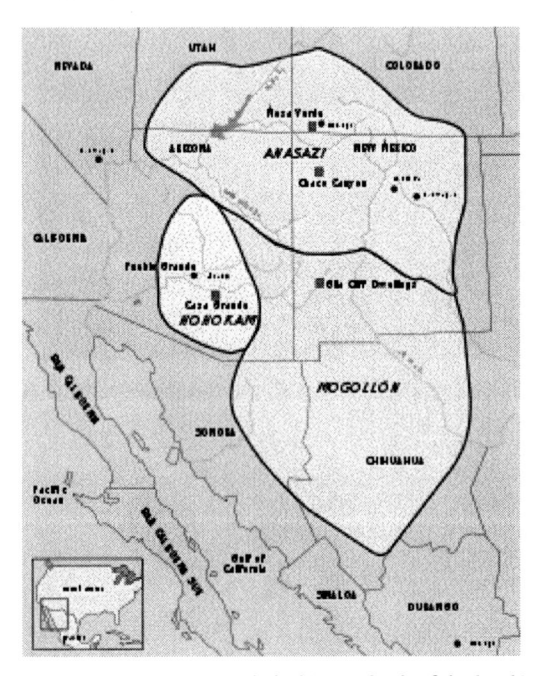

Anasazi territory shown in light brown (back of the book).

The Ancient Pueblo were one of four major prehistoric archaeological traditions recognized in the American Southwest. The others are the Mogollon, Hohokam and Patayan. In relation to neighboring cultures, the Ancient Pueblo occupied the northeast quadrant of the area. The Ancient Pueblo homeland centers on the Colorado Plateau, but extends from central New Mexico on the east to southern Nevada on the west. Areas of southern Nevada, Utah and Colorado form a loose northern boundary, while the southern edge is defined by the Colorado and Little Colorado rivers in Arizona and the Rio Puerco and Rio Grande in New Mexico. However, structures and other evidence of Ancient Pueblo culture has been found extending east onto the American Great Plains, in areas near the Cimarron and Pecos rivers and in the Galisteo Basin.

Terrain and resources within this massive region vary greatly. The plateau regions are generally high, with elevations ranging from 4500 to 8,500 feet (2,600 m). Extensive horizontal mesas are capped by sedimentary formations and support woodlands of junipers, pinon, ponderosa pines, and yellow pines, each favoring different elevations. Wind and water erosion have created steep walled canyons, and sculpted windows and bridges out of the sandstone landscape. In areas where erosionally resistant strata (sedimentary rock layers) such as sandstone or limestone overlie more easily eroded strata such as shale, rock overhangs formed. These overhangs were favored sites for shelters and building sites. All areas of the Ancient Pueblo homeland suffered from periods of drought and wind and water erosion. Summer rains could be undependable and often arrived in destructive thunderstorms. While the amount of winter snowfall varied greatly, the Ancient Pueblo depended on the snow for most of their water. Snow melt allowed the germination of seeds, both wild and cultivated, in the spring. Where sandstone layers overlay shale, snow melt could accumulate and create seeps and springs, which the Ancient Pueblo used as water sources. Snow also fed the smaller, more predictable tributaries, such as the Chinle, Animas, Jemez and Taos rivers. The larger rivers were less important to the ancient culture, as smaller streams were more easily diverted or controlled for irrigation.

Pueblo Bonito, the largest of the Chacoan Great Houses, stands at the foot of Chaco Canyon's northern rim.

The Ancient Pueblo culture is perhaps best-known for the stone and adobe dwellings built along cliff walls, particularly during the Pueblo II and Pueblo III eras. Adobe structures are constructed with bricks created from sand, clay, and water, with some fibrous or organic material, shaped using frames and dried in the sun. The best-preserved examples of the stone and adobe dwellings are in National Parks (USA), parks such as Chaco Canyon or Chaco Culture National Historical Park, Bandelier National Monument, Mesa Verde National Park, Hovenweep National Monument, and Canyon de Chelly National Monument. These villages, called pueblos by Spanish settlers, were often only accessible by rope or through rock climbing.

However, these astonishing building achievements had more modest beginnings. The first Ancestral Puebloan homes and villages were based on the pit-house, a common feature in the Basketmaker periods.

Ancestral Puebloans are also known for their pottery. In general, pottery ware used for cooking or storage in the region was unpainted gray, either smooth or textured. In the northern or "Anasazi" portion of the Ancestral Pueblo world, from about 500 to 1300 AD, the most common decorated pottery had black painted designs on white or light gray backgrounds. Decoration is characterized by fine hatching, and contrasting colors are produced by the use of mineral-based paint on a chalky background. Some tall cylinders are considered ceremonial vessels while narrow-necked jars may have been used for liquids. Ware in the southern portion of the region, particularly after A.D. 1150, is characterized by heavier black-line decoration and the use of carbon-based colorants. In northern New Mexico, the local "black on white" tradition, the Rio Grande white wares, continued well after 1300 AD.

Changes in pottery composition, structure and decoration are signals of social change in the archaeological record. This is particularly true as the peoples of the American Southwest began to leave their traditional homes and migrate south. According to archaeologists Patricia Crown and Steadman Upham, the appearance of the bright colors on Salada Polychromes in the 14th century may reflect religious or political alliances on a regional level. Late 14th and 15th century pottery from central Arizona, widely traded in the region, has colors and designs which may derive from earlier ware by both Anasazi and Mogollon peoples. (Cordell, p. 142-143)

The Ancestral Puebloans also created many petroglyphs (**Petroglyphs** (also called rock engravings) are images created by removing part of a rock surface by incising, pecking, carving, and abrading. Outside North America, scholars often use terms such as "carving", "engraving", or other descriptions of the technique to refer to such images. Petroglyphs are found world-wide, and are often (but not always) associated with prehistoric peoples) and pictographs (a **pictograph** *pictogram* or *pictogramme*) is an ideogram that conveys its meaning through its pictorial resemblance to a physical object. Earliest examples of pictographs include ancient or prehistoric drawings or paintings found on rock walls. Pictographs are also used in writing and graphic systems in which the characters are to considerable extent pictorial in appearance. Pictography is a form of writing which uses representational, pictorial drawings. It is a basis of cuneiform and, to some extent, hieroglyphic writing, which uses drawings also as phonetic letters or determinative rhymes).

The period from 700-1130 AD saw a rapid increase in population due to consistent and regular rainfall patterns. Studies of skeletal remains show that this growth was due to increased fertility rather than decreased mortality. However, this tenfold increase in population over the course of a few generations could not be achieved by increased birthrate alone; likely it also involved migrations of peoples from surrounding areas. Innovations such as pottery, food storage, and agriculture enabled this rapid growth. Over several decades, the Ancient Pueblo culture spread across the landscape. Ancient Pueblo culture has been divided into three main areas or branches, based on geographical location: Chaco Canyon (northwest New Mexico), Kayenta (northeast Arizona), and Northern San Juan (or Mesa Verde) (southwest Colorado).

Modern Pueblo oral traditions hold that the Pueblo originated to the north of their current settlements, from Shibapu, where they emerged from the underworld. For unknown ages they were led by war chiefs guided by the Spirits across North America. They settled first in the Ancient Pueblo areas for a few hundred years, then migrated to their current location.

Ancestral Puebloan ruins in Dark Canyon Wilderness, Utah

It is not entirely clear why the Ancestral Puebloans migrated from their established homes in the 12th and 13th centuries. Factors examined and discussed include global or regional climate change (Little Ice Age), prolonged periods of drought, cyclical periods of topsoil erosion, environmental degradation, de-forestation, hostility from new arrivals, religious or cultural change, and even influence from Mesoamerican cultures. Many of these possibilities are supported by archaeological evidence.

Current opinion holds that the Ancestral Puebloans responded to pressure from Numic-speaking peoples moving onto the Colorado Plateau as well as climate change which resulted in agricultural failures. The archaeological record indicates that it was not unusual for ancient Pueblo peoples to adapt to climatic change by changing residences and locations. Early Pueblo I sites may have housed up to 600 individuals in a few separate but closely spaced settlement clusters. However, they were generally occupied for a mere 30 years or less. Archaeologist Timothy A. Kohler excavated large Pueblo I sites near Dolores, Colorado, and discovered that they were established during periods of above-average rainfall. This would allow crops to be grown without benefit of irrigation. At the same time, nearby areas experiencing significantly drier patterns were abandoned.

The ancient Pueblos attained a cultural "Golden Age" between about 900 and 1130. During this time, generally classed as Pueblo II, the climate was relatively warm and rainfall mostly adequate. Communities grew larger and were inhabited for longer periods of time. Highly specific local traditions in architecture and pottery emerged, and trade over long distances appears to have been common. Domesticated turkeys appear. After approximately 1150, North America experienced significant climatic change in the form of a 300 year drought called the Great Drought, which also led to the collapse of the Tiwanaku civilization around Lake Titicaca. The contemporary Mississippian culture also collapsed during this period. Confirming evidence is found in excavations of the western regions of the Mississippi Valley between 1150 and 1350, which show long-lasting patterns of warmer, wetter winters and cooler, drier summers. In this later period, the Pueblo II became more self-contained, decreasing trade and interaction with more distant communities. Southwest farmers developed irrigation techniques appropriate to seasonal rainfall, including soil and water control features such as check dams and terraces. However, the population of the region continued to be mobile, abandoning settlements and fields under adverse conditions.

Along with this change in precipitation patterns, there was a drop in water table levels due to a different cycle unrelated to rainfall. This forced the abandonment of settlements in the more arid or over-farmed locations.

Evidence also suggests a profound change in religion in this period. Chacoan and other structures constructed originally along astronomical alignments, and thought to have served important ceremonial purposes to the culture, were systematically dismantled. Doorways were sealed with rock and mortar. Kiva walls show marks from great fires set within them, which probably required removal of the massive roof—a task which would require significant effort. Habitations were abandoned, tribes split and divided and resettled far elsewhere. This evidence suggests that the religious structures were deliberately abandoned slowly over time. Puebloan tradition holds that the ancestors had achieved great spiritual power and control over natural forces, and used their power in ways that caused nature to change, and caused changes that were never meant to occur. Possibly, the dismantling of their religious structures was an effort to symbolically undo the changes they felt they caused due to their abuse of their spiritual power, and thus make amends with nature.

Most modern Pueblo peoples (whether Keresans, Hopi, or Tanoans) and historians such as James W. Loewen, in his book *Lies Across America: What Our Historic Markers and Monuments Get Wrong* (1999), assert the ancient Pueblo did not "vanish" as is commonly portrayed in media presentations or popular books, but migrated to areas in the southwest with more favorable rainfall and dependable streams. They merged into the various Pueblo peoples whose descendants still live in Arizona and New Mexico. This perspective is not new and was also presented in reports from early 20th century anthropologists, including Frank Hamilton Cushing, J. Walter Fewkes and Alfred V. Kidder. Many modern Pueblo tribes trace their lineage from settlements. For example, the San Ildefonso Pueblo people believe that their ancestors lived in both the Mesa Verde and the Bandelier areas. Evidence also suggests that a profound change took place in the Anasazi area and areas inhabited by their cultural neighbors, the Mogollon.

Stress on the environment may have been reflected in the social structure, leading to conflict and warfare. Near Kayenta, Arizona, Jonathan Haas of the Field Museum in Chicago has been studying a group of Ancient Pueblo villages that relocated from the canyons to the high mesa tops during the late

1200s. The only reason Haas can see for a move so far from water and arable land is defense against enemies. He asserts that isolated communities relied on raiding for food and supplies, and that internal conflict and warfare became common in the 13th century. This conflict may have been aggravated by the influx of less settled peoples, Numic-speakers such as the Utes, Shoshones and Piutes, who may have originated in what is today California.

A 1997 excavation at Cowboy Wash near Dolores, Colorado, found remains of at least twenty-four human skeletons that showed evidence of violence and dismemberment, with strong indications of cannibalism. This modest community appears to have been abandoned during the same time period. (LeBlanc, p. 174) Other excavations within the Ancient Pueblo culture area produce varying numbers of unburied, and in some cases dismembered, bodies. This evidence of warfare, conflict, and cannibalism is hotly debated by some scholars and interest groups. Suggested alternatives include: a community under the pressure of starvation or extreme social stress, dismemberment and cannibalism as religious ritual or in response to religious conflict, the influx of outsiders seeking to drive out a settled agricultural community via calculated atrocity, or an invasion of a settled region by nomadic raiders who practiced cannibalism; such peoples have existed in other times and places; e.g. the Androphagi of Europe (**Androphagi** was an ancient nation of cannibals north of Scythia (according to Herodotus), probably in the forests between the upper waters of the Dnepr and Don. These people may have assisted the Scythians when King Darius the Great let a Persian invasion into what is now Southern Russia to punish the Scythians for their raids into the Persian Empire).

The term "Anasazi" was established in archaeological terminology through the Pecos Classification system in 1927. Archaeologist Linda Cordell discussed the word's etymology and use:

The name "Anasazi" has come to mean "ancient people," although the word itself is Navajo, meaning "enemy ancestors." [The Navajo word is *anaasází* (<*anaa*—"enemy", *sází* "ancestor").] The term was first applied to ruins of the Mesa Verde by Richard Wetherill, a rancher and trader who, in 1888-1889, was the first Anglo-American to explore the sites in that area. Wetherill knew and worked with Navajos and understood what the word meant. The name was further sanctioned in archaeology when it was adopted by Alfred V. Kidder, the acknowledged dean of Southwestern Archaeology. Kidder felt that it was less cumbersome than a more technical term he might have used. Subsequently some archaeologists who would try to change the term have worried that because the Pueblos speak different languages, there are different words for "ancestor," and using one might be offensive to people speaking other languages.

However, some translations of "Anasazi" suggest a translation closer to "ancestors that are now scattered", perhaps referring to a diaspora or exodus. Some modern Pueblo peoples object to the use of the term *Anasazi*, although there is still controversy among them on a native alternative. Some modern descendants of this culture often choose to use the term "pueblo peoples". The modern Hopi use the word "*Hisatsinom*" in preference to Anasazi.

However, Navajo Nation Historic Preservation Department (NNHPD) spokesperson Ronald Maldonado has indicated the Navajo do not favor use of the term "Ancestral Puebloan." In fact, reports submitted for review by NNHPD are rejected if they include use of the term.

David Roberts, in his book "In Search of the Old Ones: Exploring the Anasazi World of the Southwest", explained his reason for using the term "Anasazi" over a term using "Puebloan", noting that the latter term "derives from the language of an oppressor who treated the indigenes of the Southwest far more brutally than the Navajo ever did."

Mesa Verde National Park is a U.S. National Park and UNESCO World Heritage Site located in Montezuma County, Colorado. The park occupies 81.4 square miles (211 km^2) (211 square kilometers) near the Four Corners and features numerous ruins of homes and villages built by the ancient Pueblo people known as the Anasazi. The Anasazi made this stone village their home in the 1200s AD. It is best known for several spectacular cliff dwellings—structures built within caves and under outcroppings in cliffs—including Cliff Palace, which is thought to be the largest cliff dwelling in North America. The Spanish term *Mesa Verde* translates into English as "green table".

Mesa Verde National Park is located in the lower south-western corner of the state of Colorado.

Elevations in the park range from about 6,100 to 8,400 feet (1,900 to 2,600 m). The terrain in much of the park is dominated by ridges and valleys running roughly north and south; many of these ridges peak at an east-west crest near the park's northern border which turns more northerly-southerly towards the park entrance. The northernmost point is 13.2 miles (21.2 kilometers) farther north than the southernmost; the westernmost point is 11.9 miles (19.2 kilometers) farther west than the easternmost.

Although explorers from Spain went through the general region in the 18th century, actual sight of the cliffs dwellings by outsiders seems to have first occurred in the latter half of the 19th century. The fame of Mesa Verde soon began to spread thanks to the Wetherill ranchers and the archeological work of Gustaf Nordenskiöld. Vandalism led to the President Teddy Roosevelt's support of protecting the area as a national park in 1906.

Spanish explorers seeking a route from Santa Fe to California in the 1760s and 1770s were the first Europeans to reach the Mesa Verde (*green table*) region, which they named after its high, tree-covered plateaus. But they never got close enough, or into the needed angle, to see the ancient stone villages, which would remain a secret for another century.

Occasional trappers and prospectors visited, with one prospector, John Moss, making his observations known in 1873. The following year he led eminent photographer William Henry Jackson through Mancos Canyon, at the base of Mesa Verde. There Jackson both photographed and publicized a typical stone cliff dwelling. In 1875 geologist William H. Holmes retraced Jackson's route. Reports by both Jackson and Holmes were included in the 1876 report of the Hayden Survey, one of the four federally financed efforts to explore the American West. These and other publications led to proposals to systematically study Southwestern archaeological sites. They did not lead to action for some years.

Meanwhile, ranchers were beginning to settle the Mancos Valley. Some climbed up into Mesa Verde and observed more and larger stone structures. Looting of artifacts began, both for home display and for sale cheaply to visitors to the region. In a dismal two decades of despoliation, the most responsible ranchers were members of the Wetherill family, who also had the best relations with the local Ute tribe on whose territory Mesa Verde was located. The Wetherills collected artifacts for sale to the Historical Society of Colorado as well as private collectors, and began assembling a small library of relevant publications. They also saw the tourist potential of the cliff dwellings they now sought out systematically. Over several years they reoriented their ranch toward guiding tourists through the cliff dwellings, and became the first experts on them. Although they continued to dig in the ruins, knocking down some walls and roofs and gathering artifacts without extensive documentation, the Wetherill's actions were more responsible and considerate than those of the other looters that preceded them. Modern archaeological opinion generally agrees that the Wetherill family were reasonable caretakers in an era before archaeological standards and federal oversight and protection.

House of Many Windows.

One noteworthy early visitor was a New York newspaper reporter named Virginia McClurg, whose efforts over a period of years helped lead eventually to park status for Mesa Verde. Another, in 1889 and 1890, was photographer and travel writer Frederick H. Chapin. He described the landscape and structures in an 1890 article and 1892 book, *The Land of the Cliff-Dwellers*, whose many excellent photographs were the first extensive view of Mesa Verde available to the public. Like other visitors in the early years, he was guided by the Wetherills.

Perhaps the most important early visitor was Gustaf Nordenskiöld, son of Finnish-Swedish polar explorer Adolf Erik Nordenskiöld, in 1891. Nordenskiöld, a trained mineralogist, introduced scientific methods to artifact collection, recorded locations, photographed extensively, diagrammed sites, and correlated what he observed with existing archaeological literature as well as the home-grown expertise of the Wetherills.

The Cliff Palace in 1891, *photo by Gustaf Nordenskiöld*.

Local opposition surfaced, however, and, after it was learned that Nordenskiöld's artifacts would be shipped to a museum in northern Europe, he was arrested and charged with "devastating the ruins." Rumors of lynching circulated. Only intervention by several Washington cabinet secretaries freed Nordenskiöld.

On return to Sweden, Nordenskiöld published, in 1893, the first scholarly study of the ruins, *The Cliff Dwellers of the Mesa Verde*, which put Mesa Verde on the map in the international community. Nordenskiöld's activities remained controversial for many decades but are generally recognized as highly valuable today. Nordenskiöld's collection of Mesa Verde artifacts—in the National Museum of Finland is the largest outside the U.S. Former Mesa Verde National Park superintendent Robert Heyder summed up Nordenskiöld's contributions:

The Cliff Palace today.

I shudder to think what Mesa Verde would be today had there been no Gustaf Nordenskiöld. It is through his book that the cliff dwellings of Mesa Verde became known and his volume might well be called the harbinger of Mesa Verde National Park as we know it today.

Yet vandalism continued. By the end of the 19th century, it was clear that Mesa Verde needed protection from unthinking or greedy people. An early Mesa Verde National Park superintendent, Hans Randolph, described the situation at the best known cliff dwelling, Cliff Palace:

Parties of "curio seekers" camped on the ruin for several winters, and it is reported that many hundred specimens therefrom have been carried down the mesa and sold to private individuals. Some of these objects are now in museums, but many are forever lost to science. In order to secure this valuable archaeological material, walls were broken down . . . often simply to let light into the darker rooms; floors were invariably opened and buried kivas mutilated. To facilitate this work and get rid of the dust, great openings were broken through the five walls which form the front of the ruin. Beams were used for firewood to so great an extent that not a single roof now remains. This work of destruction, added to that resulting from erosion due to rain, left Cliff Palace in a sad condition.

Spruce Tree House.

Long view of Spruce Tree House.

As concern grew over the archaeological well being of Mesa Verde's ruins, and those in other nearby sites, the area was established as a national park on June 29, 1906. As with all historical areas administered by the National Park Service, the park was listed on the National Register of Historic Places on October 15, 1966. It was designated a World Heritage Site on September 6, 1978. The park was named with the Spanish for *green table* because of its forests of juniper and piñon trees.

A set of six buildings built by the National Park Service in 1921, the Mesa Verde Administrative District, was designated a National Historic

Landmark on May 29, 1987. It consists of the first buildings constructed by the National Park Service which are based on cultural traditions represented in the park area. The principal designer believed that structures could be used for interpretive purposes to explain the construction of prehistoric dwellings in the Park, and be compatible with their natural and cultural setting.

In the summers of 2000 (twice), 2001, 2002, and 2003, the park, which is covered with pinyon pine and utah juniper forests, suffered from a large number of forest fires; parts of it were closed. All areas of the park have since re-opened, but some areas show significant damage from the fires.

Mesa Verde's park entrance is about 9 miles (15 kilometers) east of the community of Cortez. The visitor center is 15 miles (24 kilometers) from the entrance, and Chapin Mesa (the most popular area) is another 6 miles (10 kilometers) beyond the visitor center.

The park's Chapin Mesa Archeological Museum provides information about the Ancient Puebloan civilization and displays findings and artwork.

Park Ranger giving a tour at Mesa Verde National Park.

Three of the cliff dwellings on Chapin Mesa are open to the public. Spruce Tree House is open all year, weather permitting. Balcony House and Cliff Palace are open except in the winter; visitors may tour them only on ranger-guided tours. The cliff dwellings on Wetherill Mesa, including Long House and Step House, can be reached via a 12 mile (19.2 kilometer) long mountain road leading southwest from the park visitor center. Many other dwellings are visible from the road but not open to tourists.

In addition to the cliff dwellings, Mesa Verde boasts a number of mesa-top ruins. Examples open to public access include the Far View Complex, Cedar Tree Tower, and the Sun Temple, all on Chapin Mesa, and Badger House Community, on Wetherill Mesa.

Also in the park are hiking trails, a campground, and facilities for food, fuel, and lodging; these are unavailable in the winter.

The Mesa Verde National Park Post Office has the ZIP Code 81330.

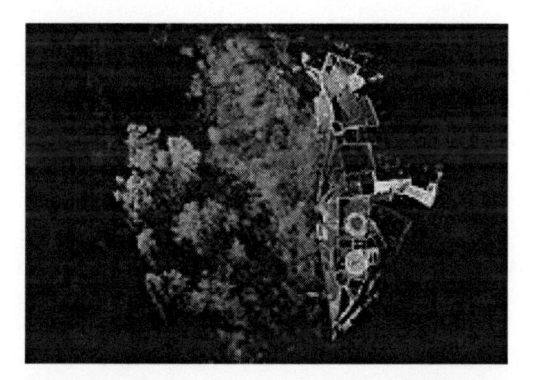

Plan of entire Spruce Tree House from above, cut from a Laser scan.

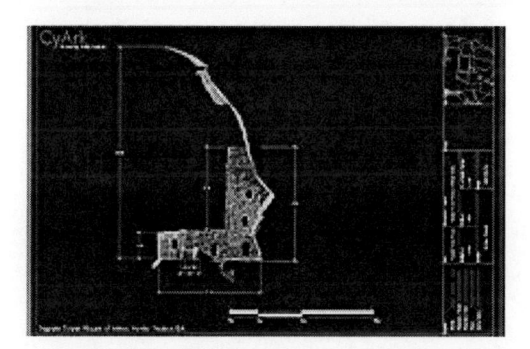

Laser scan section of the four-story Square Tower House.

Mesa Verde is best known for a large number of well preserved *cliff dwellings*, houses built in shallow caves and under rock overhangs along the canyon walls. The structures contained within these alcoves were mostly blocks of hard sandstone, held together and plastered with adobe mortar. Specific constructions had many similarities, but were generally unique in form due to the individual topography of different alcoves along the canyon walls. In marked contrast to earlier constructions and villages on top of the mesas, the cliff dwellings of Mesa Verde reflected a region-wide trend towards the aggregation of growing regional populations into close, highly defensible quarters during the 1200s.

While much of the construction in these sites conforms to common Pueblo architectural forms, including Kivas, towers, and pit-houses, the space constrictions of these alcoves necessitated what seems to have been a far denser concentration of their populations. Mug House, a typical cliff dwelling of the period, was home to around 100 people who shared 94 small rooms and eight kivas built right up against each other and sharing many of their walls; builders in these areas maximized space in any way they could and no areas were considered off-limits to construction.

Not all of the people in the region lived in cliff dwellings; many colonized the canyon rims and slopes in multi-family structures that grew to unprecedented size as populations swelled. Decorative motifs for these sandstone/mortar constructions, both cliff dwellings and non-, included T-shaped windows and doors. This has been taken by some archaeologists, such as Stephen Lekson (1999), as evidence of the continuing reach of the Chaco Canyon elite system, which had seemingly collapsed around a century before. Other researchers see these motifs as part of a more generalized Puebloan style and/or spiritual significance, rather than evidence of a continuing specific elite socioeconomic system.

Overhead view of Square Tower House.

Round tower, Cliff Palace. Photo by Ansel Adams, 1941.

Mesa Verde from a northern view, May, 2007.

Photo of a modern visitor next to the hand holds used to reach the mesa top by the original inhabitants of Cliff Place.

For most of the 12th and 13th centuries, known archaeologically as the Classic Period, the Ancient Puebloan Native Americans lived in the cliff dwellings. The reason for their sudden departure about 1275 remains unexplained; theories range from crop failures due to droughts to an intrusion of foreign tribes from the North.

Main article: Cliff Palace

This ruin is the largest and best-known of the cliff dwellings in Mesa Verde. The site has 150 identified rooms and 23 kivas (A **kiva** is a room used by modern Puebloans for religious rituals, many of them associated with the kachina belief system. Among the modern Hopi and most other Pueblo peoples, kivas are square-walled and underground, and are used for spiritual ceremonies). Although this and other Mesa Verde sites are large and well constructed, they demonstrate a long history of occupation and their architectural design is an aggregation of dwellings and storage spaces that developed slowly and randomly. Accurate archaeological information from this site has been limited due to several decades of digging and collecting at the turn of the Twentieth century.

This ruin situated on Wetherill Mesa was professionally excavated in the late 1960s by archaeologist Arthur Rohn. The structure contains 94 rooms, in four levels, including a large kiva, with simple vertical walls and masonry pilasters. This ceremonial structure has a keyhole shape, due to a recess behind the fireplace and a deflector, that is considered an element of the Mesa Verde style. The rooms clustered around the kiva formed part of the courtyard, indicating the kiva would have been roofed.

Located on Chapin Mesa, this cliff dwelling is easily accessible and well preserved. The ruins include a kiva with a restored roof which visitors can enter. Excavations indicate that this structure, like many other dwellings in Mesa Verde, was probably occupied for less than a century.

The tower that gives this site its name is the tallest structure in Mesa Verde. This cliff dwelling was occupied between AD 1200 and 1300.

These ancient reservoirs, built by the Ancient Puebloans, were named a National Civil Engineering Historic Landmark on September 26, 2004.

Records indicate that the Balcony House was probably first rediscovered by an excavator, S.E. Osborn, sometime in 1884—his name and the date "March 20, 1884" being found in a dwelling nearby. Furthermore, Osborn published a newspaper account of dwellings, including one that matches the description of Balcony House, in 1886. The site was excavated by archaeologist Jesse Nusbaum in 1910.

In February 2008, the *Colorado Historical Society* has decided to invest a part of its US$7 million budget into a Culturally modified trees project in the National Park.

Archaeological cultural units such as "Anasazi", Hohokam, Patayan or Mogollon are used by archaeologists to define material culture similarities and differences that may identify prehistoric socio-cultural units, equivalent to modern societies or peoples. The names and divisions are classification devices based on theoretical perspectives, analytical methods and data available at the time of analysis and publication. They are subject to change, not only on the basis of new information and discoveries, but also as attitudes and perspectives change within the scientific community. It should not be assumed that an archaeological division or culture unit corresponds to a particular language group or to a socio-political entity such as a tribe.

When making use of modern cultural divisions in the American Southwest, it is important to comprehend that current terms and conventions have significant limitations:

Archaeological research focuses on items left behind during people's activities: fragments of pottery vessels, garbage, human remains, stone tools or evidence left from the construction of dwellings. However, many other aspects of the culture of prehistoric peoples are not tangible. Their beliefs and behavior are difficult to decipher from physical materials, and their languages remain unknown as they had no known writing system.

Cultural divisions are tools of the modern scientist, and so should not be considered similar to divisions or relationships the ancient residents may have recognized. Modern cultures in this region, many of whom claim some of these ancient people as ancestors, contain a striking range of diversity in lifestyles, social organization, language and religious beliefs. This suggests the ancient people were also more diverse than their material remains may suggest.

The modern term "style" has a bearing on how material items such as pottery or architecture can be interpreted. Within a people, different means to accomplish the same goal can be adopted by subsets of the larger group. For example, in modern Western cultures, there are alternative styles of clothing that characterized older and younger generations. Some cultural differences may be based on linear traditions, on teaching from one generation or "school" to another. Other varieties in style may have distinguished between arbitrary groups within a culture, perhaps defining status, gender, clan or guild affiliation, religious belief or cultural alliances. Variations may also simply reflect the different resources available in a given time or area.

Defining cultural groups, such as the Ancient Pueblo peoples, tends to create an image of territories separated by clear-cut boundaries, like border boundaries separating modern states. These simply did not exist. Prehistoric people traded, worshipped, collaborated and fought most often with other nearby groups. Cultural differences should therefore be understood as "clinal", "increasing gradually as the distance separating groups also increases". Departures from the expected pattern may occur because of unidentified social or political situations or because of geographic barriers. In the Southwest, mountain ranges, rivers and, most obviously, the Grand Canyon can be significant barriers for human communities, likely reducing the frequency of contact with other groups. Current opinion holds that the closer cultural similarity between the Mogollon and Ancient Pueblos and their greater differences from the Hohokam and Patayan is due to both the geography and the variety of climate zones in the Southwest.

Puebloan peoples:

Taos Pueblo, circa 1920

The **Pueblo people** are a Native American people in the Southwestern United States. Their traditional economy is based on agriculture and trade. When first encountered by the Spanish in the 16th century, they were living in villages that the Spanish called *pueblos*, meaning "villages". Of the 21 pueblos that exist today, Taos, Acoma, Zuni, and Hopi are the best-known.

Spanish colonization of the Americas:

The Spanish colonization of the Americas was the exploration, conquest, settlement and political rule over much of the western hemisphere. It was initiated by the Spanish *conquistadors* and developed by the Monarchy of Spain through its administrators and missionaries with auxiliaries, for the real needs of wealth and trade and perceived need of indigenous conversions, that existed for a period of over four hundred years.

Beginning with the 1492 arrival of Christopher Columbus, over nearly four centuries the Spanish Empire would expand across: most of present day Central America, the Caribbean islands, and Mexico; much of the rest of North America including the Southwestern, Southern coastal, and California Pacific Coast regions of the United States; and though inactive, with claimed territory in present day British Columbia Canada; and U.S. states of Alaska, Washington, and Oregon; and the western half of South America. In the early 19th century the wars of independence liberated all the Spanish colonies in the Americas, except for Cuba and Puerto Rico later in 1898. Spain's loss of the last two in the Spanish-American War politically ended Spanish colonization in the Americas. The cultural influences remain.

Spanish Colonization:

The expansion of Spanish colonization of the Americas during the 18th century.

Christopher Columbus:

Portuguese explorers sailing caravels were establishing new routes southward along the coast of West Africa, with reaching the rich trading regions of Asia by sea, sailing east, probable.

Christopher Columbus attempted to persuade King John II of Portugal *(João II)* to sponsor an expedition, unsuccessfully. Columbus was persuasive with *Los Reyes Católicos* (the Catholic Monarchs), recently crowned Isabella I Queen of Castile and her husband Ferdinand II King of Aragon, to sponsor his novel idea: to reach Asian trade centers by sailing West across the Atlantic Ocean.

Columbus arrived on the island of Guanahani in the Bahamas on his first voyage in 1492. He encountered the indigenous Arawak people there. In his journal Columbus wrote, "I could conquer the whole of them with fifty men and govern them as I please". He imprisoned ten to twenty-five native people and took them back to Spain, with seven or eight surviving. He presented the Spanish monarchs with small items of gold, parrots, and other 'exotic' things. They commissioned Columbus for a second voyage, providing him with seventeen ships, nearly 1,500 men, cannons, crossbows, guns, cavalry, and attack dogs. He returned to claim the island of Hispaniola, present day Haiti and the Dominican Republic, from the indigenous Taíno people in 1493.

Columbus was granted governorship of the new territories and made more journeys across the Atlantic Ocean. While generally regarded as an excellent navigator, during this first stay in the New World, Columbus wrecked his flagship, the Santa Maria. He was a poor administrator and was stripped of the governorship in 1500.

He profited by using the labour of native slaves for agriculture and to mine gold. He attempted to sell native people as slaves in Spain, bringing five hundred people back. The Taínos began to resist the Spanish, refusing to plant and abandoning captured native villages. Over time the rebellion grew violent. In the resulting conflict, the native inhabitants used their extensive knowledge of the terrain and applied guerilla tactics such as booby traps, ambushes, attrition, and forced marches to tire the Spanish columns. Although stone arrows couldn't penetrate the best of the Spanish armor, they were somewhat effective if they were used as shrapnel, since they tended to shatter on impact; stone and copper maces were used more effectively. In 1522, a Taíno Cacique named Enriquillo waged a successful rebellion causing the Spaniards to sign a treaty granting the Indian population the rights of Freedom and of Possession. It had little consequence however, as by then the Taíno population was rapidly declining from to European diseases, forced labour, and ritual suicides. The Taíno often refused to participate in activities forced upon them by the Spanish which resulted in suicide. Their children were killed as a perceived escape from a terrible future.

On his fourth and final voyage to America in 1502, Columbus encountered a large canoe off the coast of what is now Honduras filled with trade goods. He boarded the canoe and found cacao beans, copper and flint axes, copper bells, pottery, and colorful cotton garments. This was the first contact of the Spanish with the civilizations of Central America.

First mainland explorations:

In 1513, Vasco Núñez de Balboa crossed the Isthmus of Panama, and led the first European expedition to see the Pacific Ocean from the west coast of the New World. In an action with enduring historical import, Balboa claimed the Pacific Ocean and all the lands adjoining it for the Spanish Crown. It was 1517 before another expedition from Cuba explored Central America. It landed on the coast of the Yucatán peninsula in search of slaves.

First settlement in the Americas:

The first mainland explorations were followed by a phase of inland expeditions and conquest. The Spanish crown extended the Reconquista effort, completed in Spain in 1492, to non-Catholic people in new territories. In 1502 on the coast of present day Colombia, near the Gulf of Urabá, Spanish explorers led by Vasco Núñez de Balboa explored and conquered the area near the Atrato River. The conquest was of the Chibchan speaking nations, mainly the Muisca and Tairona indigenous people that lived here. The Spanish founded San Sebastian de Uraba in 1509—abandoned within the year, and in 1510 the first permanent mainland settlement in the Americas, Santa María la Antigua del Darién. These were the first European settlements in the Americas.

The first permanent European, and Spanish, settlement on the mainland of the Americas was in 1510.

Mexico:

There is a difference in the 'Spanish conquest of Mexico' between the Spanish conquest of the Aztec Empire and the Spanish conquest of Yucatán. The former is conquest of the campaign, led by Hernán Cortés from 1519-21 and his Tlaxcala and other 'indigenous peoples 'allies against the Mexica/Aztec empire. The Spanish conquest of Yucatán is the much longer campaign, from 1551-1697, against the Maya peoples of the Maya civilization in the Yucatán Peninsula of present day Mexico and northern Central America. The day Hernán Cortés landed ashore at present day Veracruz, April 22, 1519, marks the beginning of 300 years of Spanish hegemony over the region.

In 1532 at the Battle of Cajamarca a group of Spanish soldiers under Francisco Pizarro and their indigenous Andean *Indian auxiliaries* native allies ambushed and captured the Emperor Atahualpa of the Inca Empire. It was the first step in a long campaign that took decades of fighting to subdue the mightiest empire in the Americas. In the following years Spain extended its rule over the Empire of the Inca civilization.

The Spanish took advantage of a recent civil war between the factions of the two brothers Emperor Atahualpa and Huascar, and the enmity of indigenous nations the Incas had subjugated, such as the Huancas, Chachapoyas, and Cañaris. In the following years the conquistadors and indigenous allies extended control over the greater Andes region. The Viceroyalty of Perú was established in 1542.

These peoples were the first to successfully revolt against the Spanish in **the Pueblo Revolt of 1680**, which expelled the Spanish for 12 years. The code for the action was a knotted rope sent by a runner to each pueblo; the number of knots signified the number of days to wait before beginning the uprising. It began August 10, 1680; by August 21, Santa Fe fell to 2,500 warriors. On September 22, 2005, the statue of Po'pay, (Popé) the leader of the Pueblo Revolt, was unveiled in the Capitol Rotunda in Washington D.C. The statue was the second one from the state of New Mexico and the 100th and last to be added to the Statuary Hall collection. It was created by Cliff Fragua, a Puebloan from Jemez Pueblo, and it is the only statue in the collection created by a Native American.

Sculptor Fragua and the unveiling the statue of Po'pay in Washington DC.

Spain's administration of its colonies in the Americas was divided into the Viceroyalty of New Spain 1535 (capital, México City), and the Viceroyalty of Peru 1542 (capital, Lima). In the 18th century the additional Viceroyalty of New Granada 1717 (capital, Bogotá), and Viceroyalty of Rio de la Plata 1776 (capital, Buenos Aires) were established from portions of the Viceroyalty of Peru.

This evolved from the Council of the Indies and Viceroyalties into an Intendant system, in an attempt for more revenue and efficiency.

19th century (the end):

During the Peninsular War in Europe between France and Spain, assemblies called *juntas* were established to rule in the name of Ferdinand VII of Spain. The Libertadores (Spanish and Portuguese for "Liberators") were the principal leaders of the Latin American wars of independence from Spain. They were predominantly *criollos* (local-born people of European, mostly of Spanish or Portuguese, ancestry), bourgeois and influenced by liberalism and in most cases with military training in the metropole (mother country).

In 1809 the first declarations of independence from Spanish rule occurred in the Viceroyalty of New Granada. The first two were in present day Bolivia at Sucre (May 25), and La Paz (July 16); and the third in present day Ecuador at Quito (August 10). In 1810 Mexico declared independence, with the Mexican War of Independence following for over a decade. In

1821 Treaty of Córdoba established Mexican independence from Spain and concluded the War. The Plan of Iguala was part of the peace treaty to establish a constitutional foundation for an independent Mexico.

These began a movement for colonial independence that spread to Spain's other colonies in the Americas. The ideas from the French and the American Revolution influenced the efforts. All of the colonies, except Cuba and Puerto Rico, attained independence by the 1820s. The British Empire offered support, wanting to end the Spanish monopoly on trade with its colonies in the Americas.

In 1898, the United States won victory in the Spanish-American War from Spain, ending the colonial era. The U.S. took occupation of Cuba, the Philippines, and Puerto Rico. The latter continues as a self-governing unincorporated territory of the United States.

The Spanish possession and rule of colonies in the Americas ended in 1898.

The **Spanish-American War** was a conflict in 1898 between Spain and the United States. Revolts had been endemic for decades in Cuba and were closely watched by Americans; there had been war scares before, as in the Virginius Affair in 1873. By 1897-98 American public opinion grew more angry at reports of Spanish atrocities, and, after the mysterious sinking of the battleship *Maine* in Havana harbor, pushed the government headed by President William McKinley, a Republican, into a war McKinley had wished to avoid. Compromise proved impossible; Spain declared war on April 23, 1898; the U.S. Congress on April 25 declared the official opening as April 21.

Although the main issue was Cuban independence, the ten-week war was fought in both the Caribbean and the Pacific and was notable for a series of one-sided American naval and military victories. The outcome by late 1898 was a peace treaty favorable to the U.S., followed by temporary American control of Cuba and indefinite colonial authority over Puerto Rico, Guam and the Philippines. Spain, whose politics had become highly unstable, managed to get rid of a very expensive empire with honor (the U.S. paid Spain $20 million). The victor gained several island possessions spanning the globe and a rancorous new debate over the wisdom of imperialism.

20th century:

In 1947 the countries of Ibero-America, Spain, and Portugal formed the *Comunidad Iberoamericana de Naciones* or 'The Organization of

Ibero—American States for the Education, Science and the Culture'. In 1948 the Organization of American States (OAS), or as it is known in the three other official languages (OEA); was founded with the goal: "to achieve an order of peace and justice, to promote their solidarity, to strengthen their collaboration, and to defend their sovereignty, their territorial integrity, and their independence."

The Union of South American Nations (USAL), Portuguese: *União de Nações Sul-Americanas*—(UNASUL), Spanish: *Unión de Naciones Suramericanas*—(UNASUR) is an intergovernmental union. It was founded in 2004 to join the existing customs unions of Mercosur and the Andean Community of Nations, continuing the process of economic integration in South America. A common currency is being discussed. USAL is modeled on the European Union.

Cultural impact:

Indigenous peoples (Native Americans)

The cultures and populations of the indigenous peoples of the Americas were changed by the Spanish assumption and colonization of their lands.

Before the arrival of Columbus, in Hispaniola the indigenous Taíno pre-contact population of several hundred thousand declined to sixty thousand by 1509. Although population estimates vary, Father Bartolomé de las Casas, the "Defender of the Indians" estimated there were 6 million (6,000,000) Taíno and Arawak in the Caribbean at the time of Columbus's arrival in 1492.

The population of the Native Amerindian population in Mexico declined by an estimated 90% (reduced to 1-2.5 million people) by the early 1600s. In Peru the indigenous Amerindian pre-contact population of around 6.5 million declined to 1 million by the early 1600s.

In California (U.S.), Sherburne F. Cook was the most persistent and painstaking student of this problem, examining in detail both pre-contact estimates and the history of demographic decline during mission and post-mission periods. The population of, between first contact in 1769 to 1821, dropped from 300,000-700,000 people to 25,000. On this Cook rendered his harshest criticism: "The first (factor) was the food supply . . . The second factor was disease . . . . A third factor, which strongly intensified the effect of the other two, was the social and physical disruption visited upon the Indian. He was driven from his home by the thousands, starved, beaten, raped, and murdered with impunity. He was not only given no assistance in the struggle against foreign diseases, but was prevented from adopting even the most elementary measures to secure his food, clothing, and shelter. The utter devastation caused by the white man was literally incredible, and not until the population figures are examined does the extent of the havoc become evident."

Missionary effort:

The Spaniards were committed, by Vatican decree, to convert their New World indigenous subjects to Catholicism. However, often initial efforts were questionably successful, as the indigenous people added Catholicism into their longstanding traditional ceremonies and beliefs. The many native expressions, forms, practices, and items of art could be considered idolatry and prohibited or destroyed by Spanish missionaries, military, and civilians. This included religious items, sculptures, and jewelry made of gold or silver, which were melted down before shipment to Spain.

Though the Spanish did not impose their language to the extent they did their religion, some indigenous languages of the Americas evolved into replacement with Spanish, and lost to present day tribal members. When more efficient they did evangelize in native languages. Introduced writing systems to the Quichua, Nahuatl and Guarani peoples may have contributed to their expansion.

Spanish emigration:

It has been estimated that in the 1500s about 240,000 Spaniards emigrated to the Americas, and in the 1600s about 500,000, predominantly to Mexico and Peru. Between the 1800s and 1940, 6 million Spaniards emigrated to Argentina, it is the second highest ethnicity. In the early 1900s impoverished Spaniards, and from the 1930s-70s political exiles from the Spanish Civil War and the Franco government, immigrated to the countries that were former colonies in the Americas—predominantly Cuba, Mexico, and Argentina. After the 1970s, the direction reversed as Hispanic Americans began settling in Spain.

Subdivisions:

While there are numerous subdivisions of Pueblo People that have been published in the literature, Kirchhoff (1954) published a subdivision of the Pueblo People into two subareas: the group that includes Hopi, Zuñi, Keres, Jemez which share exogamous matrilineal (**Matrilineality** is a system in which lineage is traced through the mother and maternal ancestors) clans, have multiple kivas, believe in emergence of people from the underground, have four or six directions beginning in the north, and have four and seven as ritual numbers. This group stands in contrast to the Rammal-speaking Pueblos (except Jemez) who have nonexogamous patrilineal clans, two kivas or two groups of kivas and a general belief in dualism, emergence of people from underwater, five directions beginning in the west, and ritual numbers based on multiples of three.

Eggan (1950) in contrast, posed a dichotomy between Eastern and Western Pueblos, based largely on subsistence differences with the Western or Desert Pueblos of Zuñi and Hopi dry-farmers and the Eastern or River Pueblos irrigation farmers. They mostly grew corn.

Linguistic differences between the Pueblos point to their diverse origins. The Hopi language is Uto-Aztecan; Zuñi is a language isolate; Keresan is a dialect continuum that includes Acoma, Laguna, Santa Ana, Zia, Cochiti, Santo Domingo, San Felipe. The Tanoan is an areal grouping of three branches of the Kiowa-Tanoan family consisting of 6 languages: Towa (Jemez), Tewa (San Juan, San Ildefonso, Santa Clara, Tesuque, Nambe, Pojoaque, and Hano); and the 3 Tiwa languages Taos, Picuris, and Southern Tiwa (Sandia, Isleta).

History of Pueblos:

The Pueblos are believed to be descended from the three major cultures that dominated the region before European contact:

> Mogollon, an area near the Gila Wilderness
> Hohokam, archaeological term for a settlement in the Southwest
> Ancient Pueblo Peoples (or the Anasazi a term coined by the Navajos).

Despite forced conversions to Catholicism by the Spanish, the Pueblo tribes have been able to maintain much of their traditional lifestyle. There are now some 35,000 Pueblo Indians, living mostly in New Mexico and Arizona along the Rio Grande and Colorado River.

Most of the Pueblos have annual ceremonies that are open to the public. One such ceremony is the Pueblo's feast day, held on the day sacred to its Roman Catholic patron saint (These saints were assigned by the Spanish missionaries so that each Pueblo's feast day would coincide with a traditional ceremony.) Some Pueblos also have ceremonies around the Christmas and at other times of the year. The ceremonies usually feature traditional dances outdoors accompanied by singing and drumming, interspersed with non-public ceremonies in the kivas. They may also include a Roman Catholic Mass and processions.

Formerly, all outside visitors to a public dance would be offered a meal in a Pueblo home, but because of the large number of visitors, such meals are now by personal invitation only.

Culture:

A Zuni drying platform for maize and other foods, with two women crafting pottery beneath it. From the Panama-California Exposition San Diego, California. January 1915.

Pueblo prayer included substances as well as words; one common prayer material was ground-up maize—white cornmeal. Thus a man might bless his son, or some land, or the town by sprinkling a handful of meal as he uttered a blessing. Once, after the 1692 re-conquest, the Spanish were prevented from entering a town when they were met by a handful of men who uttered imprecations and cast a single pinch of a sacred substance.

The Puebloans employed *prayer sticks*, which were colorfully decorated with beads, fur, and feathers; these prayer sticks (or *talking sticks*) were also used by other nations.

By the 1200s, Puebloans used turkey feather blankets for warmth. Cloth and weaving were known to the Puebloans before the conquest, but it is not known whether they knew of weaving before or after the Aztecs. But since clothing was expensive, they did not always dress completely until after the conquest, and breechcloths were not uncommon.

Corn was a staple food for the Pueblo people. They would use pottery to hold their food and water.

Religion:

The most highly developed Native communities of the Southwest were large villages or pueblos at the top of the mesas, or rocky tableland typical to the region. The archetypal deities appear as visionary beings who bring blessings and receive love. A vast collection of myths, defines the relationships between man, nature, plants and animals. Man depended on the blessings of children, who in turn depended on prayers and the goddess of Himura. Children led the religious ceremonies to create a more pure and holy ritual.

Hopi mythology:

The **Hopi** maintain a complex religious and mythological tradition stretching back over centuries. However, it is difficult to definitively state what all Hopis as a group believe. Like the oral traditions of many other societies, Hopi mythology is not always told consistently and each Hopi mesa, or even each village, may have its own version of a particular story. But, "in essence the variants of the Hopi myth bear marked similarity to one another." It is also not clear that those stories which are told to non-Hopis, such as anthropologists and ethnographers, represent genuine Hopi beliefs or are merely stories told to the curious while keeping safe the Hopi's more sacred doctrines. As folklorist Harold Courlander states, "there is a Hopi reticence about discussing matters that could be considered ritual secrets or religion-oriented traditions." David Roberts continues that "the secrecy that lies at the heart of Puebloan [including Hopi] life . . . long predates European contact, forming an intrinsic feature of the culture." In addition, the Hopis have always been willing to assimilate foreign ideas into their cosmology if they are proven effective for such practical necessities as bringing rain. As such, the Hopi had at least some contact with Europeans beginning the 16th century, and some believe that European Christian traditions may have entered into Hopi cosmology at some point. Indeed,

Spanish missions were built in several Hopi villages starting in 1629 and were in operation until the Pueblo Revolt of 1680. However, after the revolt, it was the Hopi alone of all the Pueblo tribes who kept the Spanish out of their villages permanently, and regular contact with whites did not begin again until nearly two centuries later. The Hopi mesas have therefore been seen as "relatively unacculturated" at least through the early twentieth century, and it may be posited that the European influence on the core themes of Hopi mythology was slight.

New Mexico Pueblos:

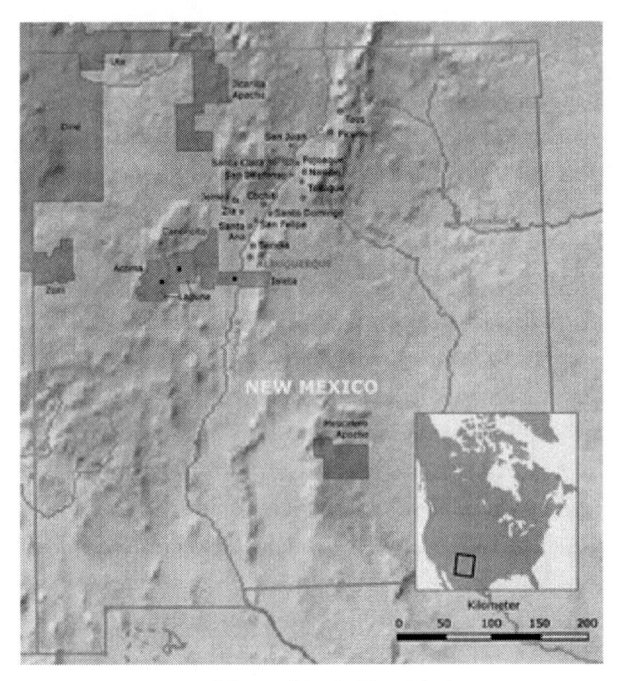

Some of the pueblos in New Mexico.

Acoma Pueblo—Keres language speakers. Oldest continuously inhabited village in US. Access to mesa-top pueblo by guided tour only (available from visitors' center), except on Sept 2nd (feast day). Photography by $10 permit per camera only. Photographing of Acoma people allowed only with individual permission. No photography permitted in Mission San Esteban del Rey or of cemetery. Sketching prohibited. Video recording strictly prohibited. Video devices will be publicly destroyed if used.

Acoma Pueblo:

Acoma Pueblo and its reflection in a pool of water.
Ansel Adams, c.1941.

Mission San Esteban Rey, c.1641. Photo by Ansel Adams, c.1941.

More recent view of the same building: architectural modifications are apparent.

Reproduction of an Acoma seed pot. Seeds were stored inside, and the pots broken as needed.

History:

The pueblo, believed to have been established in the 12th century or earlier, was chosen in part because of its defensive position against raiders. It is regarded as one the oldest continuously inhabited communities in the United States, along with Old Oraibi, Arizona, as both communities were settled in the 11th century. Access to the pueblo is difficult as the faces of the mesa are sheer (a topographic map shows this best). Before modern times access was gained only by means of a hand-cut staircase carved into the sandstone.

There are several interpretations of origin of the name "Acoma". Some believe that the name **Acoma** comes from the Keresan words for the *People of the White Rock*, with *aa'ku* meaning *white rock*, and *meh* meaning *people*. Others believe that the word *aa'ku* actually comes from the word *haaku* meaning *to prepare*; a description that would accurately reflect the defensive position of the mesa's (table top mountain) inhabitants.

Acoma Pueblo comprises several villages including Acomita, McCarty's, Anzac and the newer subdivision of Sky Line. Acoma people dry-farm in the valley below Aa'ku and use irrigation canals in the villages closer to the Rio San Jose.

In 1598, Spanish conquistador Don Juan De Oñate, under orders from the King of Spain, invaded New Mexico, and began staging raids on Native American pueblos in the area, taking anything of value. Upon reaching San Juan Pueblo, Oñate had all the Native Americans who were living there removed from their homes and used it as a base to stage more raids on other

Native American pueblos in the area. In response, the Acoma fought back, and several Spaniards were killed in the battle to re-take the pueblo from the Spaniards. During the battle, the Spaniards brought a small cannon up the back of Acoma Mesa, and began firing into the village.

According to Acoma oral traditions, the average Spaniard at the time weighed much more than the average Acoma, and the Spaniards also brought with them attack dogs, which were believed to be fed on human flesh and trained to eat humans alive. The Acoma people lost the Battle of Acoma, and the indigenous population of the pueblo, which had been approximataly 2,000 people before the Spanish attacked, was reduced to approximately 250 survivors; as women, children, and elders were killed by the Spaniards in that battle as well.

After the survivors were herded to Santo Domingo Pueblo, all the surviving children under the age of 12 were taken from their parents, and given to Spanish missionaries to raise; but most of them and the other survivors were sold into slavery. Of the few dozen Acoma men of fighting age still alive after the battle. Oñate ordered the right foot chopped off of each one. Oñate was later tried and convicted of cruelty to Indians and colonists, and was banished from New Mexico. However, he was cleared of all charges on appeal and lived out the rest of his life in Spain.

Culture:

Tracing their lineage to the inhabitants of ruins to the west and north, the Acoma people continue the traditions of their ancestors. Acoma people practice their traditional religion and some also practice the Catholic religion that came with Spanish settlers in the 1500s. Acoma people have traded and interacted with their neighbors for centuries, some of which extended beyond the local Pueblos. Trade between Aztec and Mayan people was common prior to European settlement. Only more recently has trade and interaction with other tribes been hampered by international boundaries. Traditional alliances still exist between the Pueblos who often speak different dialects or different languages. The Acoma Pueblo and Laguna Pueblo have many ties, including location, language and a shared high school. Throughout the year feasts are held in celebration of historic occasions. Visitors are allowed to attend these feasts but are encouraged to be respectful and aware of local protocol.

The Spanish settlers had the mission church of San Esteban del Rey built at the pueblo from 1629 to 1641, under the direction of Friar Juan

Ramírez. Its 30-foot beams were carried 30 miles from *Kaweshtima* or Mount Taylor Mountain, and the dirt for its graveyard was carried up the mesa from the valley below. Both the mission and the pueblo are registered National Historical Landmarks. In late 2006 the Acoma Pueblo was also named as a National Trust Historic Site.

Like other pueblos, Acoma and the surrounding area are considered federal trust land, administered by the federal government for the pueblo. Several families still live on the mesa itself year-round, while others elect to live in nearby villages (Acomita Village, New Mexico, among them). The 2000 US Census lists 2,802 inhabitants of the Acoma Pueblo and off-reservation trust lands, which encompasses territory in parts of Cibola, Socorro, and Catron counties.

Today Acoma's culture is practiced almost the same as before the 1589 invasion. The traditions are always oral traditions, in which dancing, music, art, theology, astrology, philosophy and history are taught. The traditional foods that are planted there are beans, pumpkins, corn, chili, onions and fruits like apples, apricots, peaches, plums and cherries. All of the sowing is done as a group.

The pueblo is located 60 miles (100 km) west of Albuquerque on Interstate 40 and 12 miles (20 km) south on Indian Route 23. The pueblo is open to the public only by guided tour. Photography of the pueblo and surrounding lands is restricted. Tours can be arranged and $10 camera permits obtained from the recently renovated Sky City visitor center at the base of the mesa. However, videotaping, drawing and sketching are prohibited, with big signs warning visitors not to do any of them (but especially not to videotape).

Language:

The Acoma people speak a Keresan language (this language family is a linguistic isolate).

Cochiti Pueblo:

Flag

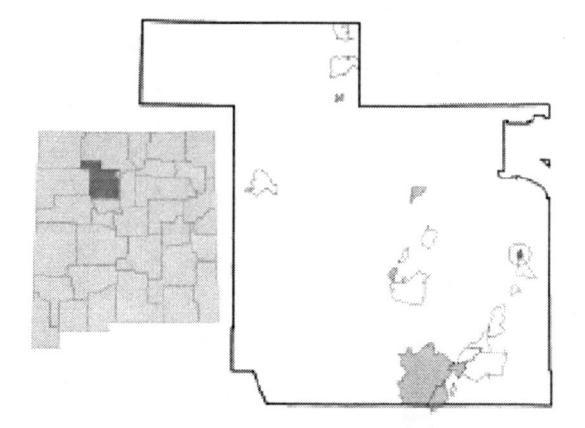

Location of Cochiti, New Mexico.

Aiyowitsa, a young woman from Cochiti Pueblo, circa 1925?

Located 22 miles (35 km) south of Santa Fe.

The pueblo celebrates the annual feast day for its patron saint, San Buenaventura, in July.

Isleta Pueblo:

House at Isleta Pueblo.

Isleta Pueblo is an unincorporated Tanoan pueblo in Bernalillo County, New Mexico, United States, originally established around the 14th century.

Isleta's new tribal casino, 2008

Social organization

Isleta (as well as Sandia) have matrilineal non-exogamous corn groups which are connected with directions and colors, a moiety system (one moiety connected with the winter, the other with the summer), a kiva system.

Kachina cults are also found in Isleta, but this being more characteristic of Western Pueblos may have been introduced by Laguna people in more recent times.

History:

The name *Isleta* is Spanish for "little island". The Spanish Mission of San Agustín de la Isleta was built in the pueblo in 1612 by Spanish Catholic Franciscans. During the Pueblo Revolt of 1680, many of the pueblo people fled to Hopi settlements in Arizona, while others followed the Spanish retreat south to El Paso del Norte (present-day El Paso, Texas. After the rebellion, the Isleta people returned to the Pueblo, many with Hopi spouses. Later in the 1800s, friction with members of Laguna Pueblo and Acoma Pueblo, who had joined the Isleta community, led to the establishment of the satellite settlement of Oraibi. Today, as well as the main pueblo, Isleta includes the small communities of Oraibi and Chicale.

Today, the pueblo operates the Isleta Casino & Resort, Isleta Eagle Golf Course and Isleta Lakes Recreational Complex.

Cultural references

Isleta is mentioned in Willa Cather's 1927 novel *Death Comes for the Archbishop*, Book Three Chapter 1. The houses are described as white inside and outside.

Jemez Pueblo:

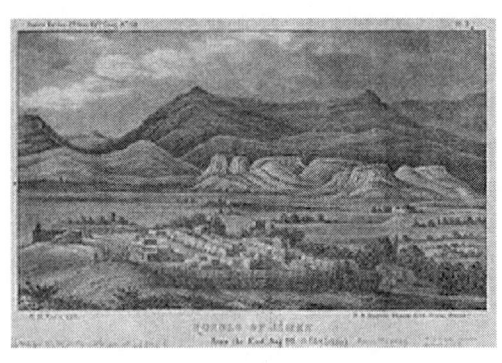

ZIP code 87024, Area code 575

According to the United States Census Bureau, the CDP has a total area of 5.3 km². There is no water on this piece of land.

Jemez Artists:

Cliff Fragua, Jemez Pueblo sculptor.

Kathleen Wall, Jemez Pueblo ceramic sculptor

Jemez Pueblo jar, by B. Tosa

As much as 70% of the 1,890 Jemez People were living on their reservation lands in the early 1970s. Though by then an increasing number were switching to wage-earning work rather than agriculture, the residents continued to raise chili peppers, corn, and wheat, to speak their native language, and to maintain customary practices.

Running, an old Jemez pastime and ceremonial activity, grew even more popular than it had been before World War II. Prior to the advent of television at Jemez, tales of running feats had been a major form of entertainment on winter nights. Races continued to hold their ceremonial place as the years passed, their purpose being to assist the movement of the sun and moon or to hasten the growth of crops, for example. At the same time, they became a popular secular sport. The year 1959 saw the first annual Jemez All-Indian Track and Field Meet, won by runners from Jemez seven times in the first ten years. A Jemez runner, Steve Gachupin, won the Pikes Peak Marathon six times, in 1968, setting a record by reaching the top in just 2 hours, 14 minutes, 56 seconds.

Jemez Pueblo—Towa language speakers. Photography and sketching prohibited at pueblo, but welcomed at Red Rocks.

Laguna Pueblo:

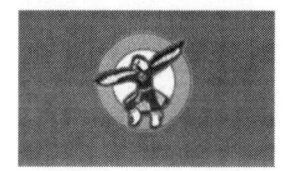

Pueblo of Laguna Symbol.

Laguna Man and Woman in Traditional Dress.

Laguna Mission, 1934. Photo: Historic American Buildings Survey.

Door to Baptistry, Laguna Mission, 1934.

An Indian Pueblo Laguna New Mexico by Thomas Moran.

Laguna (Western Keres: **Kawaik**) is a Native American tribe of the Pueblo people in west-central New Mexico, USA. The name, Laguna, is Spanish (meaning "lake") and derives from the lake located on their reservation. The real Keresan name of the tribe is "Kawaik." The population of the tribe exceeds 7,000 (enrollment), making it the largest Keresan speaking tribe. Mission San José de la Laguna was erected by the Spanish at the old pueblo (now Old Laguna), finished around July 4, 1699.

The Laguna people value intellectual activity and education, so a scholarship program has led to many well-educated Lagunas. Uranium mining on Pueblo of Laguna land has contributed to this scholarship program as well as to skilled labor learning among Laguna members. While many Native Americans love basketball, Lagunas and other Pueblos enjoy baseball. Like many Pueblos, the Laguna people are skilled in pottery.

Laguna Construction Company, a construction company owned by the Pueblo of Laguna, is one of the largest U.S. contractors in Iraq, with reconstruction contracts worth more than $300 million since 2004. In addition to its headquarters at the pueblo, Laguna Industries, Inc. maintains offices in Albuquerque, New Mexico; San Antonio and Houston, Texas; Baghdad, Iraq, and Amman, Jordan. In 2007, Laguna Construction employed 75 people, most of whom belong to the pueblo.

The Ácoma Pueblo and Pueblo of Laguna have many ties, including location, language and a shared high school.

The Pueblo of Laguna has a well-established Tribal Law system. The Pueblo of Laguna has participated as a "Weed and Seed" tribe. This Department of Justice program studied the enforcement of law and effectiveness of social programs on Native American lands.

Their reservation, lies in parts of four counties: In descending order of included land area they are Cibola, Sandoval, Valencia and Bernalillo Counties. It includes the six villages of Encinal, Laguna, Mesita, Paguate, Paraje and Seama, and had a total population of 3,815 persons as of the 2000 census. The reservation is 45 miles (75 km) west of the city of Albuquerque. The total land area is 2,013.008 km² (777.227 sq mi).

The Irish surname *Riley* was adopted by many members of the Laguna tribe in the 1800s, for legal use in Anglo culture, while retaining their Laguna names in tribal use.

Education

Primary and middle-school education is provided by the Laguna Department of Education, which also operates Early Childhood program and adult education programs. The high school is shared with nearby Acoma Pueblo.

Lagunas speak a Keresan language. (This language family is a linguistic isolate).

Laguna Pueblo—Keres speakers. Ancestors 3000 BC, established before the 14th century. Church July 4, 1699. Photography and sketching prohibited on the land, but welcomed at San Jose Mission Church.

Laguna Development Corporation

The **Laguna Development Corporation**; founded in 1998, is a wholly owned subsidiary of the Pueblo of Laguna. Laguna Development is a federally chartered tribal corporation formed under Section 17 of the 1934 Indian Reorganization Act.

The company develops and operates the tribe's retail-based outlets, including two travel centers, a supermarket, a convenience store, an RV park, an arcade, a Superette and three casinos on the Pueblo of Laguna reservation that spans Cibola County, Bernalillo, *Valencia* and *Sandoval* counties.

Several Laguna Pueblo businesses are along tourist and truck route corridors that attract New Mexico tourists, long—and short-haul truck drivers, and residents of nearby Albuquerque. Other Laguna Development businesses provide basic services to local tribal communities.

Nambé Pueblo:

Located 20 miles (30 km) north of Santa Fe at the base of the Sangre de Cristo Mountains, Nambé means "People of the round Earth" in the Tewa language, and the pueblo people are from the Tewa ethnic group of Native Americans. The Pueblo of Nambé has existed since the 14th century and was a primary cultural, economic, and religious center at the time of the arrival of Spanish colonists in the very early 17th century. Nambé was one of the Pueblos that organized and participated in the Pueblo Revolt of 1680. Nambé is known for its beautiful waterfalls and a distinctive style of pottery, known as Nambé normie. The *Feast Day* for Nambé Pueblo is October 4. Nambé is a member of the Eight Northern Pueblos.

Nambe Pueblo—Tewa language speakers. Established in the 14th century. Was an important trading center for the Northern Pueblos. Nambe is the original Tewa name, and means "People of the Round Earth". Feast Day of St. Francis October 4th.

Ohkay Owingeh Pueblo:

Ohkay Owingeh potters at work, 1937. Pottery making was historically important in the economy of San Juan, and continues today at Ohkay Owingeh.

Ohkay Owingeh is a pueblo in Rio Arriba County. Its elevation is 5,663 feet (1,726 m) and it is located 25 miles (40 km) north of Santa Fe.

Ohkay Owingeh was previously known as **San Juan Pueblo** until returning to its pre-Spanish name in November 2005. The Tewa name of the pueblo means "place of the strong people.

Ohkay Owingeh has the ZIP code 87566 and the United States Postal Service prefers that name for addressing mail, but accepts the alternative name San Juan Pueblo. This ZIP Code Tabulation Area (ZCTA) had a population of 3,357 at the 2000 Census. The entire pueblo has a population of 6,748.

The pueblo was founded around 1200 CE. By tradition, the Tewa people moved here from the north, perhaps from the San Luis Valley of southern Colorado.

After taking control of the pueblo in 1598, the Spanish conquistador Don Juan de Oñate renamed the pueblo San Juan de los Caballeros after his patron saint, John the Baptist. He then established the first Spanish capital of New Mexico nearby.

Ohkay Owingeh is the headquarters of the Eight Northern Indian Pueblos Council, and the pueblo people are from the Tewa ethnic group of Native Americans. This is one of the largest Tewa language-speaking pueblos. The **Eight Northern Pueblos** of New Mexico are Taos, Picuris, Santa Clara, San Juan, San Ildefonso, Nambé, Pojoaque, and Tesuque.

The annual Pueblo Feast Day is June 24. The tribe owns the OhKay Casino and the Oke-Oweenge Crafts Cooperative, which showcases redware pottery, weaving, painting, and other artwork from the eight northern pueblos.

Many of the members of the Ohkay Owingeh pueblo live in San Juan, New Mexico, a few miles north.

Notable natives:

Esther Martinez, linguist and storyteller
Popé (Po-pay), the Tewa leader of the Pueblo Revolt of 1680

, May 2005

Dancers at Ohkay Owingeh.  Buffalo Dance.

Statue of Popé, Ohkay Owingeh.

Ohkay Owingeh Pueblo—Tewa speakers. Originally named O'ke Oweenge in Tewa. Headquarters of the Eight Northern Indian Pueblos Council. Home of the Popé, one of the leaders of the August 1680 Pueblo Revolt. Known as San Juan Pueblo until November 2005.

Picuris Pueblo:

San Lorenzo de Picurís, circa 1915.

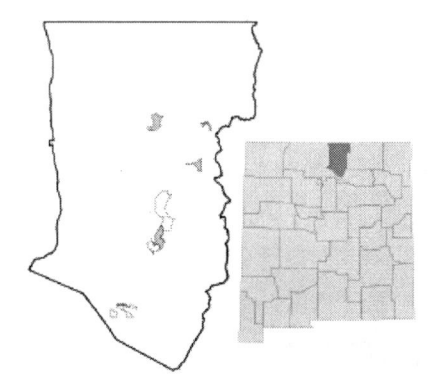

Location of Picuris Pueblo (County of Tao), New Mexico.

Picuris village has occupied its present location since around 750 CE. The Picuris people previously lived in an earlier, larger village now known as Pot Creek, near Taos, on the western slopes of the Sangre de Cristo Mountains.

Spanish explorer Don Juan de Oñate called them "pikuria"—those who paint.

According to the United States Census Bureau, the CDP has a total area of 0.4 square miles (1.2 km²), all of it land.

The **Pueblo of the Picuris** is a federally recognized tribe, whose headquarters is in Penasco, New Mexico. Their own name for their pueblo is *Pinguiltha*, meaning "mountain warrior place" or "mountain pass place." They speak the Picuris language, a dialect of the Northern Tiwa language, part of the Kiowa-Tanoan language family. Their tribal officers, led by a tribal governor, are elected every two years.

In 1990, 147 of the 1,882 enrolled tribal members lived in the pueblo; however, the number was reduced to 86 in 2000.

In 1991, the tribe opened the four-star Hotel Santa Fe and the Amaya Restaurant, serving Native American cuisine, in Santa Fe, New Mexico.

Picuris is known for its micaceous pottery. Anthony Durand (1956-2009), is a micaceous potter. Their major feast day is San Lorenzo's Day on August 10.

Pojoaque Pueblo:

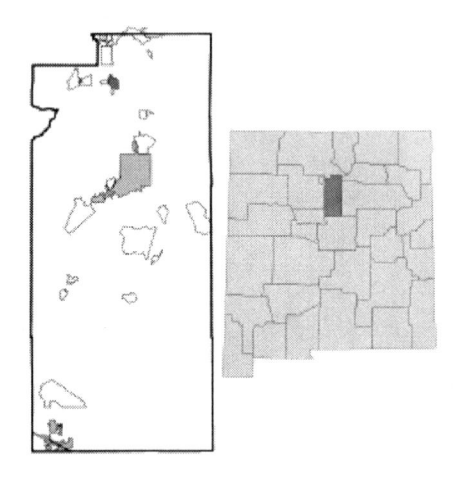

Location of Pojoaque, New Mexico.

Pojoaque is a census-designated place (CDP) in Santa Fe County. It is part of the Santa Fe, New Mexico Metropolitan Statistical Area. The population was 1,261 at the 2000 census. Pojoaque and **Pojoaque Pueblo** are neighboring communities. Pojoaque Pueblo is an Indian Reservation, and the town of Pojoaque is a collection of communities near the Pueblo with people from various ethnic backgrounds.

Highway overpass at Pojoaque.

Pojoaque Pueblo is one of the six Tewa-speaking Rio Grande Pueblos, and a member of the Eight Northern Pueblos. The Pueblo was settled around 500 AD, with the population peaking in the 15th and 16th centuries.

In the early 1600's the first Spanish mission San Francisco de Pojoaque was founded. During the Pueblo Revolt of 1680, Pojoaque was abandoned, and was not resettled until about 1706. By 1712 the population had reached 79. In about 1900, a severe smallpox epidemic caused the pueblo to be abandoned once again by 1912. In 1934, Pojoaque Pueblo was reoccupied, and became a federally-recognized Indian Reservation in 1936. Pojoaque is currently the only tribe from the 19 pueblos that hosts a dictator as government ruler.

Pojoaque Pueblo opened their new Buffalo Thunder resort in August 2008, New Mexico's largest and most expensive resort. The estimated cost for the resort project in 2004 was $250 million

The Pueblo also operates the Cities of Gold Casino, and the Poeh Museum.

Sandia Pueblo:

Sandia Resort and Casino.

Sandia Pueblo inhabiting a 101.114 km² (39.04 sq mi) reservation of the same name in the eastern Rio Grande Valley of central New Mexico, located three miles south of Bernalillo off Highway 85 in southern Sandoval County and northern Bernalillo County. It is bounded by the city of Albuquerque to the south and by the foothills of the Sandia Mountains, a landform the people hold sacred and which was central to the traditional economy and remains important in the spiritual life of the community, to the east. A forested area known as the *bosque* surrounds the rest of the reservation, and serves as a source of firewood and wild game. A resident population of 4,414 was reported as of the 2000 census. Two communities located on its territory are Pueblo of Sandia Village and part (population 3,235) of the town of Bernalillo.

A federally-recognized tribe, Sandia Pueblo is one of 19 of New Mexico's Native American pueblos. It is known as one of the state's Eastern Pueblos. Its 500 people are traditionally Tiwa speakers, a language of the Tanoan group, although retention of the traditional language has waned with later generations. They have a tribal government that operates Sandia Casino, Bien Mur Indian Market Center, and Sandia Lakes Recreation Area, as well as representing the will of the Pueblo in business and political matters.

The Tiwa name for the pueblo is **Tuf Shur Tia**, or "Green Reed Place", in reference to the green *bosque* (Spanish: *forest*). However, older documents claim that the original name of the pueblo was **Nafiat**, (Tiwa: "Place Where the Wind Blows Dust").

It became known as *Sandía* (Spanish: "watermelon") in the early seventeenth century, and possibilities abound as to why. Some claim that a type of squash cultivated there reminded the Spaniards of the melons they knew from the Easter hemisphere. Others suggest that explorers found an herb called *sandía de culebra*, or possibly another called *sandía de la pasión* there/

But the most convincing and most-cited explanation is that the Spanish called the mountain *Sandía* after viewing it illuminated by the setting sun. The Sandia Mountains have a red appearance to them, and the layer of vegetation gives it a luminous "rind" of green when backlit, giving it the appearance of a sliced watermelon. The village closest to the range took on the name of the mountain, changing from throughout the years from San Francisco de Sandía to Nuestra Señora de los Dolores de Sandía to Nuestra Señoría de los Dolores y San Antonio de Sandía before ending up as simply **Sandia Pueblo** or **Pueblo of Sandia**.

During a 1936 expedition, experienced archeologist Wesley Bliss excavated the Sandia Cave, a cave in the Sandia Mountains, and reported his findings to University of New Mexico project head Dr. Brand. Frank C. Hibben, a UNM student who had not been involved in the excavation, later worked in the cave. He reported finding a spearpoint beneath a layer of material dating more than 25,000 years old, along with the bones of camels, mastodons, and prehistoric horses. The 25,000-year age suggested by Hibben was erroneous, as the bones were carbon dated from 14,000-20,000 years ago (16,000-14,000 BCE). The published notes of Bliss and others in reference to the poor layer integrity and cross-layer contamination associated with rodent burrowing proved that Hibben's dating of historical sedimentary layers was consistently inaccurate.

Frank Hibben's claim of a Clovis point dating to more than 25,000 years ago is cited as strong evidence for the existence of a much older pre-Folsom culture in North America (as contended by the authors of the controversial *Forbidden Archaeology*). However, Hibben's publications misrepresented the initial excavation work of Wesley Bliss, who noted the proper layers, and the poor layer integrity in areas, among other findings that were erroneously misconstrued and reported by Frank Hibben to prop up his theory. Bliss did not find any of the spearpoints in the layers reported later by Hibben. It is now believed that the spearpoints were not as old as was originally reported by Hibben, and Hibben's sloppy work and false testament to man's history in North America has greatly hindered the accuracy of our understanding of prehistoric North America. Frank Hibben was generously rewarded for this falsified work, which assisted him greatly in starting his impressive career, supported by the University of New Mexico. The errors in Hibben's work were covered up for 60 years until being openly acknowledged and reported.

It is from this dig that Sandia or Sandia-type points derive their name. They appear to be the remains of the Paleo-Indian Llano or Clovis Culture. Until about CE 400-500, cultural groups residing in the area practiced the Desert Culture of migratory hunter-gatherers. At that time, agriculture and sedentary life began to take hold, although the populations present are known to have relied on older economies in times of want. Cotton, beans, squash, and maize were cultivated, and the arts of basketry and textile weaving were developed/

The Pueblo culture developed from 700-1100, characterized by its distinctive religious beliefs and practices and a large growth in population. The period from 1100-1300 CE is known as the Great Pueblo Period, and is marked by cooperation between the Pueblo peoples and the communal Great Kiva ritual. The Sandia Pueblo has resided in its current location since the

1300s, when they comprised over 20 pueblos. They were a thriving community, numbering 3,000 at the time of the arrival of Coronado in 1539.

Encounter with Westerners and life under New Spain:

Spanish conquistador Francisco Vásquez de Coronado "discovered" the Pueblo of Sandia in 1539 while on an expedition to discover the Seven Cities of Cíbola.

In 1610, Fray Esteban de Perea, known as the "Apostle of Sandia", arrived. A descendent of a distinguished Spanish family, he was Guardian, Commissary, and Custodian of the friars in New Mexico, and was responsible for the implementation of the Inquisition in the territories under his authority. The tradition of witchcraft may have led to the Holy Office's establishment.

In 1617 the area became home to the seat of the Mission of San Francisco. The Spanish exacted tribute and enslaved members of the Sandia Pueblo people for labor in the building of churches and in Mexican mines. As a result of the resentment against this abuse, the Sandia, who had already offered sanctuary for Zia and Jemez rebels, were one of the pueblos involved in the August 10, 1680 Popé-led Pueblo Revolt against Spanish rule that drove the Spanish from the region until its reconquest by Diego de Vargas in 1692. They did not find freedom, however, as Popé and his successor Luis Tupatu exacted as heavy a tribute as the Spanish and the raiding tribes had. By way of punishment for their insurrection, then governor of the territory, Antonio de Otermin, ordered the village, which by that time had been abandoned, burned on August 26. Having fled to neighboring Hopi lands, the rectory at Sandia was left unprotected and was looted.

The Sandia returned after each Spanish attack, with the 441 surviving Sandia resettling permanently in November 1742. In 1762, Governor Tomas Cachupin ordered the rebuilding of Sandia Pueblo (although his concern was primarily the housing of the Hopi who had found refuge there) as a buffer between the settlement at Albuquerque and the raids of the semi-nomadic Navajo and Apache. As a result, Sandia was raided continuously, the most deadly of such events occurring in 1775 when a Comanche raid killed thirty. The Hopi suffered the brunt of the attack as a result of their segregation from the Sandia, which has minimized their influence in the Pueblo. As a result of wars with Spanish conquistadors and raids from neighboring indigenous nations, the Sandia Pueblo diminished, numbering 350 by 1748, and dwindling to 74 by 1900.

Sandia Pueblo Governor Victor Montoya (right) meeting with Congresswoman Heather Wilson.

Rule of the territory passed to Mexican hands at the end of the Mexican War of Independence in 1820. It proved difficult to establish a new republic and govern outlying territories with a history of insubordination at the same time, and New Mexico enjoyed a brief semi-autonomous period resembling the salutary neglect of the American colonies. In American history, this period is often referred to as the "Wild West", in reference to relative absence of Mexican authority, which left the region open to incursion from and settlement by American pioneers.

With the end of the Mexican-American War in 1848, the territory of New Mexico was ceded to the United States. Zebulon Pike made note of the Sandia Mountains during his 19th century expedition, calling them the "San Dies".

When Indian schools were built in Albuquerque and Santa Fe, Sandia pupils were in attendance. Nonetheless, American culture did not have a strong effect on the tribe until World War II, when the tribe sacrificed eight of their young men to the national defense. The pueblo became electrified in 1952.

Tribal authorities have sometimes had conflicts with state and federal authorities. They have sought to assert their longstanding claim to the Sandia Mountains east of the ridge, and they strongly opposed the construction of the Sandia Peak Tramway in 1966.

The tribe opened a casino in 1994, and have since expanded and added a hotel to the facility. The casino's amphitheater hosts many acts passing through Albuquerque, and its proximity to the state's main urban center has made it a popular attraction among gamblers. The tribe has used the windfall to finance the education of their youth (i.e., every member who wants it is guaranteed a college education) and is currently financing a wastewater treatment plant. They also make contributions to several local charities. Some problems the Pueblo currently faces are alcoholism and teen pregnancy.

The tribal government has educational, police, maintenance, health and human services, environmental, and economic development departments. "A Governor, Lt. Governor, Warchief, and Lt. Warchief are appointed for annual terms according to Sandia's cultural tradition. Each man can be appointed to consecutive terms. The Governor and Warchief will become Tribal Council members for life. The Warchief and Lt. Warchief are responsible for all religious activities held in the Pueblo. The Governor oversees day to day government operations, while the Lt. Governor is the Tribal Court Judge.

The Sandia Mountains, the sacred land of the Sandia people.

Today, English is the common language of the Pueblo, although it is sprinkled with Southern Tiwa and Spanish words and expressions. Older generations speak Southern Tiwa, Spanish, and English, but younger generations have reportedly not preserved linguistic traditions as well as their elders.

Interestingly, many Spanish words incorporated into common usage, such as *horno* (Spanish for "oven") and *bosque* (Spanish for "woods"), are now pronounced with an "American" accent. (*Horno*, referring to the ceramic outdoor oven still in common use, is pronounced ['hor no] (cf. Spanish ['or no]), and *bosque* is pronounced ['bas ki] (cf. Spanish ['bos ke]).

At Sandia, Southern Tiwa is still used in music, ceremony, and daily life.

The Sandia people are known for their pottery, and sell hand-crafted arts through the Bien Mur Indian Market Center.

The Spanish reported that the Sandia people wore elegant garments adorned with turquoise. At that time, they wore their hair like the Isleta and San Ildefonso tribes. Now they dress and wear their hair like any other Americans, although there is a tendency for men to grow their hair long, as is common in the Native American community in general.

The Sandia are a deeply religious people, and to this day remain very secretive about many aspects of their religion. Early reports discuss devotion to *santos*, or effigies of saints, a syncretic phenomenon common throughout the Southwest.

Though nominally Catholic, they preserve many of their pre-Catholic traditions. Their feast day, a tradition common to all Pueblo people, is celebrated yearly on June 13. This feast, or *fiesta*, as it is called, is open to the public. Music and dance are big parts of the ceremony, and it is considered an honor to participate.

Other holy days are closed entirely, and non-Indian residents must leave (sometimes for days at a time) during these ceremonies. Personal feast days are celebrated too, with the tradition of "throwing", when gifts are thrown from rooftops to the recipients below.

The people have a deep connection to the Sandia Mountains, which they refer to as "the Mountain", and think of as their "church." They use the mountain as their official symbol.

Early documents discuss the belief in kachinas and the creation of kachina dolls, a practice that may continue. Males undergo secret initiation rituals involving the use of kivas (rooms for worship), but little else is known about the rite in the outside world.

In a tradition similar to the saying of grace, Sandia people place a bit of their meal in a receptacle in remembrance and sacrifice.

Tales of belief in and fear of witchcraft date from the earliest accounts of the pueblo.

Kachina:

Drawings of kachina dolls, from an 1894 anthropology book.

Kachina dolls in the Heard Museum in Phoenix, Arizona.

A metal statue signifying a kachina dancer at the Carefree. Resort in Carefree, Arizona:

A **kachina** (also **katchina** or **katcina**, is a spirit being in western Pueblo cosmology and religious practices. The western Pueblo, Native American cultures located in the southwestern United States, include Hopi, Zuni, Tewa Village (on the Hopi Reservation), Acoma Pueblo, and Laguna Pueblo. In later times, the kachina cult have spread to more eastern Pueblos, e.g. from Laguna to Isleta. The term also refers to the **kachina dancers**, masked members of the tribe who impersonate kachinas in religious ceremonies, and kachina dolls, wooden dolls representing kachinas which are given as gifts to children.

In Hopi, the word *qatsina* means literally "life bringer" and can be anything that exists in the natural world or cosmos. A kachina can represent anything from a revered ancestor, to an element, a location, a quality, a natural phenomenon, or a concept. There are more than 400 different kachinas in Hopi and Pueblo culture. The local pantheon of kachinas varies in each pueblo community; there may be kachinas for the sun, stars, thunderstorms, wind, corn, insects, and many other concepts. Kachinas are understood as having humanlike relationships; they may have uncles, sisters, and grandmothers, and may marry and have children. Although not worshipped, each is viewed as a powerful being who, if given veneration and respect, can use their particular power for human good, bringing rainfall, healing, fertility, or protection, for example.

The Zuni believe that the kachinas live in the Lake of the Dead, a mythical lake which is reached through Listening Spring Lake located at the junction of the Zuni River and the Little Colorado River.

Within Hopi mythology, the kachinas are said to live on the San Francisco Peaks near Flagstaff, Arizona. The most important Hopi kachinas are called *wuya*.

Among the Hopi, kachina dolls are traditionally carved by the uncles and given to uninitiated girls at the Bean Dance (Spring Bean Planting Ceremony) and Home Dance Ceremony in the summer. The function of the dolls is to acquaint children with some of the many kachinas.

In Hopi the word is often used to represent the spiritual beings themselves, the dolls, and the people who dress as kachinas for ceremonial dances, which are understood to all embody aspects of the same belief system. Among other uses, the kachinas represent historical events and things in nature, and are used to educate children in the ways of life.

The most important of the kachinas are known as *wuya*.

San Felipe Pueblo:

San Felipe Pueblo (Eastern Keres: **Katishtya**) is a census-designated place (CDP) in Sandoval County, (ZIP 87501, Area Code 505) and is located 10 miles (16 km) north of Bernalillo. As of the 2000 census, the CDP population was 2,080. It is part of the Albuquerque Metropolitan Statistical Area. The Pueblo, founded in 1706, comprises Native Americans who speak an eastern dialect of the Keresan languages.

The Pueblo celebrates the annual Feast of St. Philip on May 1, when hundreds of pueblo people participate in traditional corn dances.

Today, the tribe operates Casino Hollywood, just off Interstate 25.

San Felipe Pueblo—Keres speakers. 1706. Photography and sketching prohibited at pueblo.

San Ildefonso Pueblo:

The Pueblo is a census-designated place (CDP) in Santa Fe County. The population was 458 at the 2000 census. San Ildefonso Pueblo is a member of the Eight Northern Pueblos, and the pueblo people are from the Tewa ethnic group of Native Americans, who speak the Tewa language.

According to the United States Census Bureau, the CDP has a total area of 4.2 square miles (10.7 km²), of which, 3.9 square miles (10.2 km²) of it is land and 0.2 square miles (0.6 km²) of it (5.54%) is water.

Black Mesa.

San Ildefonso Pueblo is located at the foot of the Pajarito Plateau just 12.87 km (8 miles) east from Los Alamos, 38.6 km (24 miles) NW of Santa Fe. A large volcanic outcroping lies directly north of San Ildefonso Pueblo, it is called the "Black Mesa." The Rio Grande runs through San Ildefonso Pueblo and the lowest elevation is approximately 1676 meters (5500 feet).

The pueblo was founded when people came from the Mesa Verde complex in Southern Colorado. These people had first moved to Bandelier just south of present-day Los Alamos. There these people thrived due to the rainfall (elevation about 7000 feet) and the ease of constructing living structures from the surrounding soft volcanic rock. But after a prolonged drought, the people moved down into the valleys of the Rio Grande around 1300 AD. The Rio Grande and other arroyos (An **arroyo** (literally *brook* in Spanish), also called a **wash**, is usually a dry creek bed or gulch that temporarily fills with water after a heavy rain, or seasonally. As such, the term is similar to the word wadi. Arroyos can be natural or man-made. The term usually applies to a mountainous desert environment), provided the water for irrigation.

Black-on-Black pottery of the pueblo. Artifact at the Field Museum, Chicago.

The Spanish conquistadors tried to subdue the native people and force their religion on the native people during the early 1600s, which lead to the Pueblo Revolt of 1680. The people withstood the Spaniards by climbing to the top of the Black Mesa. The siege ended with the surrender of the native people, but the Spanish gave the native people some freedom of religion and other self-governing rights.

The pueblo natives continued to lead an agricultural based economy until the early 1900s when Maria Martinez and her husband Julian Martinez rediscovered how to make the Black-on Black pottery for which San Ildefonso Pueblo would soon become famous. From that time the pueblo has become more tourist-oriented, with numerous tourist shops existing in the Pueblo. Because of close proximity to the state capital, Santa Fe, and the presence of the Los Alamos National Laboratory, many of those employed in the pueblo have government jobs

San Ildefonso Pueblo, Santa Fe—Tewa speakers. Originally at Mesa Verde and Bandelier. The valuable black-on-black pottery was developed here by Maria and Julian Martinez. Photography by $10 permit only. Sketching prohibited at pueblo. Heavily-visited destination.

Santa Ana Pueblo:

A census-designated place (CDP) in Sandoval County. As of the 2000 census, the CDP had a total population of 479. It is part of the Albuquerque Metropolitan Statistical Area (ZIP code 87004). The Pueblo, named Tamaya in the native language, administers a total reservation land of 73,000 acres (295 km²) in the Rio Grande valley and is composed of Native Americans who speak an eastern dialect of the Keresan languages.

The pueblo celebrates an annual feast day for its patron saint, St. Anne, on July 26.

Today, the Pueblo operates the Santa Ana Star Casino and is the site of the Hyatt Regency Tamaya Resort & Spa. They also run arts & crafts, gardening and cooking enterprises.

According to the United States Census Bureau, the CDP has a total area of 7.4 square miles (19.3 km²), of which, 6.9 square miles (17.9 km²) of it is land and 0.5 square miles (1.4 km²) of it (7.11%) is water.

Santa Clara Pueblo:

(Tewa: **Kha'po**) is a census-designated place (CDP) in Rio Arriba County (ZIP code 87052). The population was 980 at the 2000 census. Santa Clara Pueblo was established about 1550. The pueblo is a member of the Eight Northern Pueblos, and the people are from the Tewa ethnic group of Native Americans who speak the Tewa language. The pueblo is on the Rio Grande, between Ohkay Owingeh (formerly San Juan Pueblo) to the north and San Ildefonso Pueblo to the south. Santa Clara Pueblo is famous for producing hand-crafted pottery, specifically blackware and redware with deep engravings. The pueblo is listed on the National Register of Historic Places. According to the United States Census Bureau, the CDP has a total area of 2.1 square miles (5.4 km²), all of it land.

Double-handled Santa Clara bowl with Awanyu design,
by Florence Browning, 1996

Santo Domingo Pueblo:

(Eastern Keres: **Kewa**) is a census-designated place (CDP) in Sandoval County, and is located 25 miles (40 km) south of Santa Fe. As of the 2000 census, the CDP population was 2,550. It is part of the Albuquerque Metropolitan Statistical Area.

The Pueblo is composed of Native Americans who speak an eastern dialect of the Keresan languages.

The Pueblo celebrates an annual feast day on August 4 to honor their patron saint, St. Dominic, where more than 2,000 pueblo people participate in traditional corn dances.

According to the United States Census Bureau, the CDP has a total area of 2.0 square miles (5.2 km²), all of it land.

Taos Pueblo:

Taos Pueblo (or Pueblo de Taos) is an ancient pueblo belonging to a Taos (Northern Tiwa) speaking Native American tribe of Pueblo people.

It is approximately 1000 years old and lies about 1 mile (1.6 km) north of the modern city of Taos. The Red Willow Creek, or Rio Pueblo, is a small stream which flows through the middle of the pueblo from its source in the Sangre de Cristo Range. A reservation of 95,000 acres (384 km²) is attached to the pueblo, and about 1,900 people live in this area.

Taos Pueblo is a member of the Eight Northern Pueblos. The Taos community is known for being one of the most secretive and conservative pueblos.

Taos Pueblo's most prominent architectural feature is a multi-storied residential complex of reddish-brown adobe divided into two parts by the Rio Pueblo. According to the Pueblo's Web site, it was probably built between 1000 and 1450 A.D. It was designated a National Historic Landmark on October 9, 1960, and in 1992 became a World Heritage Site. As of 2006, about 150 people live in it full-time.

In the Taos language, the pueblo is referred to as "the village" in either tə□otho "in the village" (tə□o-"village" +-tho "in") or tə□obo "to/toward the village" (tə□o-"village" +-bo "to, toward"). The proper name of the pueblo is □ałopháymųp'□həothəolbo "at red willow canyon mouth" (or □ałopháybo "at the red willows" for short); however, this name is more commonly used in ceremonial contexts and is less common in everyday speech.

The name *Taos* in English was borrowed from Spanish *Taos*. Spanish *Taos* is probably a borrowing of Taos tə□o-"village" which was heard as *tao* to which the plural *-s* was added although in the modern language *Taos* is no longer a plural noun. The idea that Spanish *Taos* is from *tao* "cross of the order of San Juan de los Cabelleros" (from Greek *tau*) is unlikely.

Prehistory and history:

Most archeologists believe that the Taos Indians along with other Pueblo Indians settled along the Rio Grande migrated from the Four Corners region. The dwellings of that region were inhabited by the Anasazi, and a long drought in the area in the late 1200s may have caused them to move to the Rio Grande where the water supply was more dependable.

The history of Taos Pueblo includes the plotting of the Pueblo Revolt in 1680, a siege by U.S. forces in 1847, and the return by President Nixon in 1970 of the Pueblo's 48,000 acres (194 km²) of mountain land taken by President Theodore Roosevelt and designated as the Carson National Forest early in the twentieth century. Blue Lake, which the people of the

Pueblo traditionally consider sacred, was included in this return of Taos land. The Pueblo's web site names the acquisition of the sacred Blue Lake as the most important event in its history due to the spiritual belief that the Taos natives originated from the lake itself. An additional 764 acres (3.09 km^2) south of the ridge between Simpson Peak and Old Mike Peak and west of Blue Lake were transferred back to the Pueblo in 1996.

The North-Side Pueblo is said to be one of the most photographed and painted buildings in the Western Hemisphere. It is the largest multistoried Pueblo structure still existing. It is made of adobe walls that are often several feet thick. Its primary purpose was for defense. Up to as late as 1900, access to the rooms on lower floors was by ladders on the outside to the roof, and then down an inside ladder. In case of an attack, outside ladders could easily be pulled up.

The homes in this structure usually consist of two rooms, one of which is for general living and sleeping, and the second of which is for cooking, eating, and storage. Each home is self-contained; there are no passageways between the houses. Taos Indians made little use of furniture in the past, but today they have tables, chairs, and beds. In the Pueblo, electricity, running water, and indoor plumbing are prohibited.

The pueblo wall completely encloses the village except at the entrance as a symbol of the village boundaries. Now rather short, the wall used to be much taller for protection against surrounding tribes. The river running through the pueblo serves as the primary source for drinking and cooking water for the residents of the village. In the winter, the river never completely freezes although it does form a heavy layer of ice. Because the river moves so swiftly, the ice can be broken to obtain the fresh water beneath.

Spiritual community:

Three religions are represented in the Pueblo: Christianity, the aboriginal religion, and the Native American Church. Most of the Indians are Roman Catholic. Saint Jerome, or San Geronimo, is the patron saint of the pueblo.

The deep feeling of belonging to a community, summed up in their phrase, "we are in one nest," has held the Taos people together. Both men and women are expected to offer their services or "community duties," when needed. One should be cooperative and never allow their own desires to be destructive of the community's interest. One of Taos's strongest institutions is the family. Descent on both the father and the mother's side of the family is equally recognized. Each primary family lives in a separate dwelling so when a couple gets married, they move to their own home. With relatives so near by, everyone is available to help care for the children. The elderly teach the young the values and traditions that have been handed down, which protects the integrity of the Taos culture.

Taos Pueblo images:

Taos Pueblo, 1893 illustration.

Detail of Taos Pueblo.

Taos Pueblo with Rio Pueblo in foreground

The entrance to a kiva, or room for religious rituals, at Taos Pueblo

Ancient apartment-style dwellings at the Taos Pueblo.

Taos Pueblo (1935-36) by *Helmut Naumer, Sr.*

Taos Pueblo Church (1942) by Ansel Adams

Taos Pueblo Church (2009)

Tesuque Pueblo:

Camel Rock

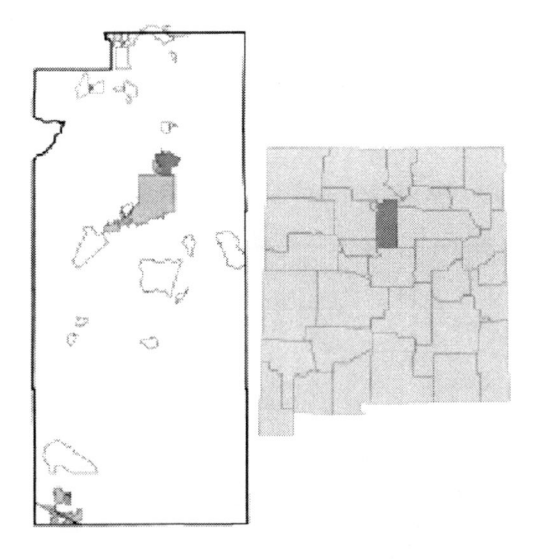

Tesuque (Tewa: Tetsuge) is a census-designated place (CDP) in Santa Fe County (Zip code 87574). It is part of the Santa Fe, New Mexico, Metropolitan Statistical Area. The population was 909 at the 2000 census. Tesuque Pueblo is a member of the Eight Northern Pueblos, and the pueblo people are from the Tewa ethnic group of Native Americans who speak the Tewa language. The pueblo was listed as a historic district on the National Register of Historic Places in 1973.

According to the United States Census Bureau, the CDP has a total area of 7.0 square miles (18.0 km²), all of it land. Camel Rock is a locally-famous and distinctive rock formation and landmark, located along U.S. Routes 84/285 across from the tribal Cities of Gold Casino.

Zia Pueblo:

Zia buffalo dancer, circa 1925. Photo: Edward S. Curtis.

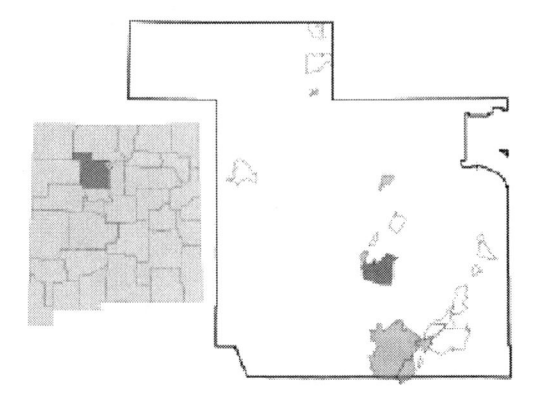

Location of Zia Pueblo (Zip code 87053).

Zia Pueblo (Eastern Keres: **Tsi'ya**, Spanish: ***Zía Pueblo***) is a census-designated place (CDP) in Sandoval County. The population was 646 at the 2000 census; Male:310 Female:336 The pueblo after which the

CDP is named is included within the CDP; it is listed on the National Register of Historic Places.

Zia Pueblo is part of the Albuquerque Metropolitan Statistical Area.

Formation on Zia Pueblo.

According to the United States Census Bureau, the CDP has a total area of 27.3 mi² (70.8 km²). 27.3 mi² (70.7 km²) of it is land and 0.04 mi² (0.1 km²) of it (0.15%) is water.

New Mexico's state flag uses the Zia symbol.

Zuni Pueblo:

Zuni Pueblo, 1850 illustration.

Location of Zuni Pueblo (ZIP Code 87327).

Zuni Pueblo (Zuni: Shiwinna, also Zuñi Pueblo and Pueblo de Zuñi) is a census-designated place (CDP) in McKinley County. The population was 6,367 at the 2000 census. It is inhabited largely by members of the Zuni people. According to the United States Census Bureau, the CDP has a total area of 8.8 square miles (22.9 km²).8.8 square miles (22.9 km²) of it is land and only a little part of the land is water.

The area is served by the nearby Black Rock Airport.

Zuni Public Schools operates schools serving the community.

The Zuni Public Library is located at 27 East Chavez Circle. In 1974 Dr. Lotsee Patterson and Ben Wakashige started a project to help tribal areas establish libraries. The Zuni library opened in 1975.

Zuni Pueblo, 1873. Timothy H. O'Sullivan, photographer.

Zuni River:

The Zuni (Zuñi) River, a tributary of the Little Colorado River, has its origin in Cibola County, New Mexico, at the Continental Divide, flowing generally in a southwesterly direction through the Zuni Indian Reservation to join the Little Colorado River in eastern Arizona. The Zuni River is approximately 90 miles in length (about 145 km).

The Zuni River is one of the last remaining habitats of the Zuni bluehead sucker.

The Zuni River is sacred to the Zuni people.

Zuni traditionally speak the Zuni language, a unique language (also called an "isolate") which is unrelated to any other Native American language. The Zuni continue to practice their traditional religion with its regular ceremonies and dances and an independent and unique belief system.

The Zuni were and are a peaceful, deeply traditional people who live by irrigated agriculture and raising stock. Their success as a desert agri-economy is due to careful management or conservation of resources as well as a complex system of community support. Many contemporary Zuni also rely on the sale of traditional arts and crafts. Some Zuni still live in the old style Pueblos, while others live in modern flat-roofed houses made from adobe and concrete block. Their location is relatively isolated, but they welcome respectful tourists.

The Zuni Tribal Fair and rodeo is held the third weekend in August. The Zuni also participate in the Gallup Inter-Tribal Ceremonial usually held in early or mid-August.

The Zuni, like other Pueblo peoples, are believed to be the descendants of the Ancient Pueblo Peoples who lived in the deserts of New Mexico, Arizona, Utah, and southern Colorado for centuries. Archaeological evidence shows they have lived in their present location for about 1300 years. However, before the Pueblo Revolt of 1680, the Zuni lived in six different villages. After the revolt, until 1692, they took refuge in a defensible position atop Dowa Yalanne, a steep mesa 5 km (3.1miles) southeast of the present Pueblo of Zuni; "Dowa" means "corn", and "yalanne" means "mountain." After the establishment of peace and the return of the Spanish, the Zuni relocated to their present location, only briefly returning to the mesa top in 1703.

In 1539, a Spanish exploratory party guided by the Moorish slave Estevanico arrived, though the villagers eventually killed him. This was Spain's first contact with any of the Pueblo peoples.

Frank Hamilton Cushing, a pioneering anthropologist associated with the Smithsonian Institution, lived with the Zuni from 1879 to 1884. He was one of the first participant observers and an ethnologist.

A controversy during early 2000s involved Zuni opposition to the development of a coal mine near the Zuni Salt Lake, a site considered sacred by the Zuni and under Zuni control. The mine would have extracted water from the aquifer below the lake and would also have involved construction between the lake and Zuni. The plan died in 2003 after several lawsuits.

Zuni Salt Lake:

Zuni Salt Lake, also Zuñi Salt Lake (Navajo: Áshįįh salt), is a rare high desert lake, and a classic maar (A **maar** is a broad, low-relief volcanic crater that is caused by a phreatomagmatic eruption, an explosion caused by groundwater coming into contact with hot lava or magma. A maar characteristically fills with water to form a relatively shallow crater lake). It is located in Catron County, about 60 miles south of the Zuni Pueblo. Zuñi Salt Lake is extremely shallow, with the depth only to four feet in the wet season. During the dry season, much of the water evaporates leaving behind saltflats. It was listed on the National Register of Historic Places in 1999.

For centuries, the Pueblo people of the Southwest, including the Zuni, Acoma, Laguna, Hopi and Taos pueblos, have made annual pilgrimages to Zuñi Salt Lake to harvest salt, for both culinary and ceremonial purposes. Ancient roadways radiate out from the lake to the various pueblos and ancient pueblo sites, such as Chaco. The lake itself is considered sacred, home of the Salt Mother deity, known to the Zuñi as Ma'l Okyattsik'i. Also known as Las Salinas to early Hispanic settlers in the area.

The Zuni Salt Lake was not part of the Zuñi reservation originally recognized by the U.S. government, but the U.S. returned the lake itself, and 5,000 acres (20 km²) surrounding it, to Zuni control in 1985.

From 1994 to 2003, there was a proposal to develop a coal mine near the Zuni Salt Lake. It would have involved extraction of water from the aquifer below the lake as well as construction between the lake and the Pueblo of Zuñi. The proposal was withdrawn after several lawsuits, and is regarded as an important exercise of native rights in the United States.

An aquifer is an underground layer of water-bearing permeable rock or unconsolidated materials (gravel, sand, silt, or clay) from which groundwater can be usefully extracted using a water well. The study of water flow in aquifers and the characterization of aquifers is called hydrogeology. Related terms include aquitard, which is a bed of low permeability along an aquifer, and aquiclude (or *aquifuge*), which is a solid, impermeable area underlying or overlying an aquifer. The surface of saturated material in an aquifer is known as the water table.

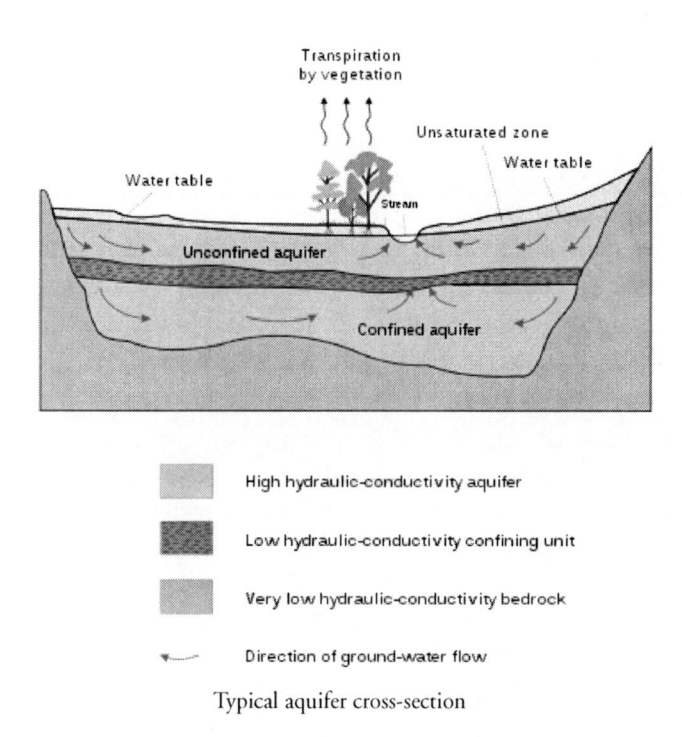

Typical aquifer cross-section

In the earlier days of that age, when Native Zuni clans roamed an area that is now the Southwestern United States, they made pottery for food and water storage. Women made pottery according to the clan's tradition of functionality and design. Clay for the pottery is sourced locally and thanks is given to the Earth Mother (*Awidelin Tsitda*) according to ritual prior to extraction. It is prepared first by grinding, and then sifting and mixing with water. After the clay is shaped into a vessel or ornament, it will be scraped smooth with a scraper. Then a thin layer of finer clay will be applied to the surface for extra smoothness. Next the vessel will be polished with a stone. Then the piece is painted with home-made organic dyes using a traditional yucca brush. The function of the ware is determined by its shape, and its design and painted images. To fire the pottery the Zuni used sheep dung in traditional kilns which had not changed for hundreds of years. However, most contemporary Zuni pottery is now fired in modern, electric kilns. While the firing of the pottery was usually a community enterprise, silence or communication in low voices was essential in order to maintain the original "voice" of the "being" of the clay and the purpose of the end product. The selling of pottery and other traditional arts and crafts is a major source of income for many of the Zuni, and an artisan may be the sole financial support for their immediate family as well as others. They made pottery, clothing, baskets.

They also make fetish carvings and necklaces for the purpose of ritual and trade, and more recently for sale to their avid collectors.

The Zuni are known for their fine silversmithing, which began in the 1870s after learning fundamental techniques from the Navajo. Lanyade was the first Zuni silversmith, who learned the art from Atsidi Chon, a Navajo smith. By 1880, Zuni jewelers already set turquoise in silver. Today jewelry making thrives as an art form in Zuni. Many Zuni have became master silversmiths and perfected the skill of stone inlay. They found that by using small pieces of stone they were able to create intricate designs and unique patterns. Small oval-shaped stones with pointed ends are set close to one another and side by side. The technique is normally used with turquoise in creating necklaces or rings. Another technique they have mastered is needlepoint.

Beliefs:

Life for these agricultural people revolves around their religious beliefs. They have a cycle of religious ceremonies which takes precedence over all else. Their religious beliefs are centered on the three most powerful of their deities—Earth Mother

A **deity** is a postulated preternatural or supernatural immortal being, who may be thought of as holy, divine, or sacred, held in high regard, and respected by believers, often called in some religions as a **god**.

A **mother goddess** is a term used to refer to any goddess associated with motherhood, fertility, creation or the bountiful embodiment of the Earth. When equated with the Earth or the natural world such goddesses are sometimes referred to as **Mother Earth** or as the **Earth Mother**.

There have been many different mother goddesses throughout history and in the present day, including such deities as the Hindu Kali Ma, ancient Greek Gaia and ancient Irish Danu. In some forms of Neopaganism, and in the Hindu idea of Shakti, all the many mother goddesses are viewed as being the embodiment of one singular deity.

Sun Father, and Moonlight-Giving Mother. The Sun is especially worshipped. In fact the Zuni words for daylight and life are the same word. The Sun is, therefore, seen as the giver of life. Each person's life is marked by important ceremonies to celebrate their coming to certain milestones in their existence. Birth, coming of age, marriage and death are especially celebrated.

Zuni religiously pilgrimage every four years on the Barefoot Trail to Kołuwala:wa, also called Zuni Heaven or Kachina Village; a 12,482-acre detached portion of the Zuni Reservation about sixty miles Southwest of Zuni Pueblo. The four-day observance occurs around the summer solstice, practiced for many hundreds of years and is well known to local residents.

Zuni pueblo in 1879.

Another pilgrimage conducted annually for centuries by the Zuni and other southwestern tribes is made to Zuni Salt Lake for the harvesting of salt during the dry months, and for religious purposes. The lake is home to the Salt Mother, Ma'l Okyattsik'i and is led to by several ancient Pueblo roads and trails.

Coming of age, or rite of passage, is celebrated differently by boys and girls. A girl who is ready to declare herself as a maiden, will go to the home of her father's mother early in the morning and grind corn all day long. Corn is a sacred food and a staple in the diet of the Zuni. The girl is, therefore, declaring that she is ready to play a role in the welfare of her people. When it is time for a boy to become a man he will be taken under the wing of a spiritual 'father', selected by the parents. This one will instruct the boy through the ceremony to follow. The boy will go through certain initiation rites to enter one of the men's societies. He will learn how to take on either religious, secular or political duties within that order.

Arizona:

Hopi Tribe Nevada-Kykotsmovi—Hopi language speakers. Area of present villages settled around 700 AD

Hopi:

The Hopi are a Native American people who primarily live on the 12,635 km² (2,531.773 sq mi) Hopi Reservation in northeastern Arizona. The Hopi Reservation is entirely surrounded by the much larger Navajo Reservation. The two nations used to share the *Navajo-Hopi Joint Use Area*. The partition of this area, commonly known as Big Mountain, by Acts of Congress in 1974 and 1996, has resulted in seemingly endless controversy.

The Hopi area according to the 2000 census has a population of 6,946 people.

The Oraibi village is the oldest Hopi village and has been occupied from at least 1150 C.E, and it has the most importance to Hopi history. It is the oldest continuously inhabited village in the United States. In the 1540s there were at least 1,500-3,000 members of the Oraibi Village.

Early European Contact, 1540-1680:

The first recorded European contact with the Hopis was by the Spanish in 1540. Spanish General Francisco Vasquez de Coronado had come to

America on an expedition to explore the land. While at the Zuni villages, he learned of the Hopi tribe. De Coronado dispatched a man named Pedro de Tovar along with other members of their regime to find these Hopi villages. The Spanish wrote that the first Hopi village they visited was Awatovi. They later noted that there were about 16,000 Hopi and Zuni people. A few years later another Spanish explorer by the name of Garcia Lopez de Cardenas came to investigate the Rio Grande and met the Hopi people. The Hopi warmly entertained de Cardenas and his men and directed him on his journey. In 1582-1583 the Hopis were visited by Antonio de Espejo's expedition. He noted that there were around five Hopi villages and around 12,000 Hopi people. During these early years, the Spanish were exploring and dominating the southwestern region of the new world. Although they were present in many other areas, there were never a large number of them in the Hopi country. Their visits to the Hopi were random and spread out over many years. Many times the visits were from military explorations The Spanish colonized near the Rio Grande and, because the Hopis didn't have any rivers to give them access to the Rio Grande, the Spanish never left any troops on their land. When they first arrived they brought with them Catholic Friars. 1629 is considered the Franciscan Period when 30 Friars came into Hopi country and created missionaries and churches at Awatovi. The Hopi Indians originally were against conversion, but after an incident where Father Porras restored the sight of a blind youth, by placing a cross over his eyes, the Hopis at Awatovi believed in Christianity. Most Hopis in the other villages continued to remain anti-Christian.

Pueblo Revolt of 1680:

The priests weren't very successful in converting the natives so they persecuted the Hopis for keeping their religion. The Spaniards also took advantage of Hopi labor and the products they produced. The harsh treatment and selfish acts of the Spanish caused the Hopis to become less tolerant of them. Out of all the Hopi Indians, only the Awatovi village disagreed with this statement. Eventually the Rio Grande Pueblo Indians suggested a revolt in the year 1680, and Hopis supported them. This was the first time that all the Pueblo Indians worked together to drive the Spanish colonists away. The Hopi people revolted against the Spanish, attacking missions, killing friars and destroying the Catholic churches that had been built. The revolt proved to be a success as the Spanish stayed out of the area of the Pueblo Indians and the Hopis until 1700. Years after the revolt, the Hopi Indians living in the village of Awatovi returned to Christianity despite the disapproval of the rest of the Hopi Villages.

Hopi-U.S Relations, 1849-1946:

In 1849, John S. Calhoun was appointed official Indian agent of Indian Affairs for the Southwest Territory of the U.S. He had a headquarters in Santa Fe and was responsible for all Indian residents of the area. The first formal meeting between the Hopi Indians and the U.S Government happened in the year 1850 when seven Hopi leaders made the trip to Santa Fe to meet with Calhoun. Their objective was to ask the government for protection against the Navajo Indians. At this time, the Hopi leader was Nakwaiyamtewa. As a result of this meeting, Fort Defiance was established in 1851 in Arizona and troops were placed in Navajo country to deal with the Navajo threats. General James J. Carleton, with the assistance of Kit Carson, was assigned to travel through the area. They "captured" the Navajo natives and forced them to the fort. As a result of the Navajo Long Walk, the Hopis were able to enjoy a short period of peace. In 1847, Mormons founded Utah and tried to convert the Indians to Mormonism. Jacob Hamlin, a Mormon missionary, first made a trip into Hopi country in 1858. He was on good terms with the Hopi Indians and in 1875 a Mormon Church was built on Hopi land.

Education:

In 1875, an English trader by the name of Thomas Keams escorted the Hopi village leaders to meet President Arthur in Washington D.C. Lololoma, acting chief at the time, was very impressed with Washington. He believed that education allowed the whites to be able to live in such a way. This belief caused him to want a school built for the Hopi children. In 1886, twenty of the Hopi leaders signed a petition sent to the Commissioner of Indian Affairs requesting that a school be built on their land. In 1887, Thomas Keams opened Keams Canyon Boarding School at Keams Canyon for the Hopi Indians. The Oraibi people were not supportive of this school. They refused to send their children to a school that was 35 miles away from their villages. The main objective of Keams School was to teach the Hopi youth the ways of civilization by pushing Anglo-American values on them. This boarding school was a way to rid the Hopis of their Indian past. The children were forced to abandon their tribal identity and completely take on the white American culture. They received haircuts, new clothes, took on a "white" name and learned English. The boys learned farming and carpentry skills, while the girls were taught ironing, sewing and "civilized" dining. Keams School also reinforced American religions. The American Baptist Home Missionary Society provided the students with services every morning and religious teachings during the week. In 1890, the Commissioner of Indian Affairs arrived in Hopi country with other government officials to investigate the progress of the new school. They saw that few students were enrolled. They later returned with federal troops who threatened to arrest the Hopi parents if they refused to send their kids to school. The parents backed down and the Commissioner took children to fill the school.

Hopi Land:

The Hopis have always viewed their land as sacred. Agriculture is a very important part of their culture and their villages are spread out across the northern part Arizona. The Hopi and the Navajos both never knew of land boundaries, including state boundaries, and just lived on the land that their ancestors did. On December 16, 1882 President Chester Arthur passed an executive order creating a reservation for the Hopi Indians. Their reservation was much smaller than the Navajo reservation, which was the largest in the country. The Hopi reservation was originally a perfect rectangle 55 by 70 miles, in the middle of the Navajo Reservation with their village lands only taking up about half of the land within their reservation. This reservation kept white settlers from coming through their land, but it did not protect the Hopis against the Navajos. Significant amount of time has been spent between the Hopi and the Navajos fighting over land. Eventually the Hopis went before the Committee of Interior and Insular Affairs to ask them to help provide a solution to the dispute between the two tribes. The tribes argued over around 1.8 million acres of land in northern Arizona. In 1887 the U.S Government passed the Dawes Allotment Act. The purpose of this Act was to divide up tribal land into privately owned individual family plots of 640 acres or less. The remaining land would be free for U.S citizens to purchase. For the Hopis, this Act would destroy their ability to farm, which was their main means of income. Fortunately the attempt of the

Bureau of Indian Affairs to set up land allotments in the Southwest never resulted in the division of Hopi land.

Oraibi Split:

The history of the Oraibi split is one of the most famous about the Hopi tribe. The chief of the Oraibi at this time, Lololoma, was very enthusiastic regarding Hopi education but the Oraibi people were divided on this issue. Most of the village was conservative and refused to allow their children to attend school. These Indians were referred to as the "hostiles" because they opposed the American government and their attempts at assimilation. The rest of the Oraibi Hopis were called the "friendlies" because of their liberal attitude and acceptance of the white people. The "hostiles," unlike the "friendlies," refused to let their children attend school. In 1893, the Oraibi Day School was opened in the Oraibi village. Even though this school was within the village, the hostile parents still refused to allow their children to attend. In 1894, a group of Hopi parents announced that they were against the ideas of Washington and did not want their children to be exposed to the culture of the White American people. They also said that this argument couldn't be settled peacefully, so the government sent in troops to arrest the nineteen parents and sent them to Alcatraz Prison where they stayed for a year. Another main Oraibi figure at this time, Lomahongyoma, competed with Lololoma for village leadership. Eventually the village split in 1906 after a battle between Hostiles and Friendlies. The conservative Hostiles were forced to leave the village and form their own village, called Hotevilla.

Hopi Recognition:

At the turn of the century, the U.S Government put a policy into effect that created day schools, missionaries, provided farming assistants and physicians on every Indian reservation. This policy required that every reservation set up its own Indian-police and Tribal courts, and appoint a chief or leader who would represent their tribe within the U.S Government. In 1910 in the Census for Indians, the Hopi Tribe had a total of 2,000 members, which was the highest in 20 years. The Navajos at this time had 22,500 members and have consistently increased in population. During the early years of this century, only about 3% of Hopis lived off the reservation.

In 1924 Congress officially declared Native Americans to be U.S citizens. The Indian Reorganization Act helped the Hopis to establish a constitution for their tribe and in 1936 also helped them to create their own Tribal Council. The Preamble to the Hopi constitution states that they are a self-governing tribe, focused on working together for peace and agreements between villages in order to preserve the "good things of Hopi life." The Constitution consists of thirteen different "Articles" all with a different topic of interest. The articles cover the topics of territory, membership, and organization of their government with a legislative, executive and judicial branch. The rest of the articles discuss the twelve villages recognized by the tribe, lands, elections, Bill of Rights and more.

Hopi-Navajo Land Disputes:

From the 1940s to the 1970s, the Navajo kept moving their villages closer and closer to Hopi land, causing the Hopis to once again bring up the land issue with the U.S Government. This resulted in the establishment of "District 6" which placed a boundary around the Hopi villages on the first, second, and third mesas, thinning the reservation to 501,501 acres. In 1962 the courts issued the "Opinion, Findings of Fact and Conclusions of Law and Judgment" which stated that the U.S government did not grant the Navajos any type of permission to reside on the Hopi reservation that was declared in 1882 and that the remaining Hopi land was to be shared with the Navajos. Between 1961-1964, the Hopi tribal council signed leases with the U.S Government that allowed for companies to explore and drill for oil, gas and minerals within Hopi country. This drilling brought over 3 million dollars to the Hopi Tribe. In 1974, The Navajo-Hopi Land Settlement Act was passed and begun the Navajo-Hopi Indian Relocation Commission that made sure every Hopi and Navajo Indian living on the other's land was to be removed. In 1992, the Hopi Reservation was increased to 1.5 million acres.

Hopis Today:

The Hopi tribe today receives most of its income from natural resources. On their 1.8 million acre reservation, there is a significant amount of coal mined yearly. Today tourism is very prevalent and important to Hopi life. There is not much set up specifically for tourists with the exception of their Cultural Center and a few campgrounds. Through a grant-loan from the Economic Development Administration and some of the tribe's own money, the Hopi tribal council constructed the Hopi Cultural Center including a restaurant, motel, craft shops, museum on the Second Mesa. Before arriving, tourists must know the laws and rules of the Hopi reservation. Typically photography is prohibited, as well as participating and viewing certain tribal ceremonies. The Hopi are a relatively poor tribe and as of 1990, 45% of families fell below poverty level. The Hopi Tribal Government provides 45% of jobs and most individuals make their income from agriculture and livestock products. Because the U.S Government holds Indian owned land "in-trust," the Hopi land cannot be taxed by any state, county, city or other local governments. Although there have been controversies regarding education in the past, today the Hopis acknowledge that education is top priority for their children. The tribe has realized the need to create funds for the education. In 2000, the Hopi Tribal council, through tribal law, created the Hopi Education Endowment Fund. The HEEF, through funding, gives financial assistance to Hopi students. The mission of the HEEF is to make sure that every Hopi Indian, present and future, has a chance to graduate high school and if they wish, continue on to a higher education.

Culture:

The name Hopi is a shortened form of what these Native American people call themselves, *Hopituh Shi-nu-mu*, "The Peaceful People" or "Peaceful Little Ones". The Catholic Encyclopedia lists the name Hopi as having been derived from "Hopita", meaning those who are "peaceful ones". *Hopi* is a concept deeply rooted in the culture's religion, spirituality, and its view of morality and ethics. The Hopi religion is anti-war. To be Hopi is to strive toward this concept, which involves a state of total reverence and respect for all things, to be at peace with these things, and to live in accordance with the instructions of Maasaw, the Creator or Caretaker of Earth. The Hopi observe their traditional ceremonies for the benefit of the entire world.

Traditionally, Hopi are organized into matrilineal clans (**Matrilineality** is a system in which lineage is traced through the mother and maternal ancestors). When a man marries, the children from the relationship are members of his wife's clan. These clan organizations extend across all villages. Children are named, however, by the women of the father's clan. On the twentieth day of a baby's life, the women of the paternal clan gather, each woman bringing a name and a gift for the child. In some cases where many relatives would attend, a child could be given over forty names, for example. The child's parents generally decide the name to be used from these names. Current practice is to either use a non-Hopi or English name or the parent's chosen Hopi name. A person may also change their name upon initiation into one of the religious societies such as the Kachina society.

The Hopi still practice a complete cycle of traditional ceremonies although not all villages retain or ever had the complete ceremonial cycle. These ceremonies take place according to the lunar calendar and are observed in each of the Hopi villages. Nonetheless, like other Native American groups, the Hopi have been impacted by Christianity. The Hopi have been affected by the missionary work carried out by several Christian denominations, however, with relatively little impact on Hopi religious practices.

Traditionally the Hopi are highly skilled micro or subsistence farmers. The Hopi also interact in the wider cash economy; a significant number of Hopi have mainstream jobs; others earn a living by creating high quality Hopi art, notably the carving of Kachina dolls, the expert crafting of earthenware ceramics, and the design and production of fine jewelry, especially sterling silver.

The Hopi people:

When a child is born, they receive a perfect ear of corn and a special blanket. On the 20th day of their life, the child is taken to the mesa cliff and held facing the rising sun. When the sun touches the baby, it is given a name.

Kachinas or Kat'sinas or Qat'sinas are referenced extensively in the Hopi. Kat'sina literally means "life bringer" in Hopi. A Kat'sina can be anything: an element, a quality, a natural phenomenon, or a concept. There are over 300 to 400 different Kat'sinas. Traditionally, Kat'sina dolls, which are made by the maternal uncles, are given to young uninitiated girls at the spring Bean Ceremony and Home Dance.

82

Historic photographs of Hopi:

Hopi Women's Dance, 1879, Oraibi, Arizona

Dancer's Rock, 1879, Walpi, Arizona

Kopeli, Hopi Snake Priest.

Hopi Basket Weaver c. 1910

Photograph by Henry Peabody, Iris Nampeyo, world famous Hopi ceramist, with her work, circa

Hopi girl at Walpi. 1900, with "squash blossom" hairdo indicative of her eligibility for courtship

Nampeyo *Ceramic jar*

Black Mesa Peabody Coal controversy:

The **Black Mesa Peabody Coal controversy** arose in the 1960s in the Black Mesa plateau of the arid Four Corners region in the western United States. The plateau overlaps the reservations of the Navajo and Hopi native American tribes.

The controversy over the Black Mesa coal mine arose from an unusually generous mineral lease agreement negotiated under questionable circumstances and the Peabody Energy coal company's use and degradation of a potable source of water to transport coal it extracted from the southwestern tip of the Black Mesa in Arizona.

In 1964 Peabody Energy (then Peabody Western Coal), a publicly-traded energy company based in the mid-west signed a contract with the Navajo tribe and two years later with the Hopi tribe, allowing the company mineral rights and use of an underground aquifer. The contract offered unusually advantageous terms for Peabody and was approved despite widespread opposition and the lack of clear government authority. It was negotiated by prominent natural resources attorney John Sterling Boyden, who claimed to be representing the Hopi tribe while actually on the payroll of Peabody.

Peabody Energy pumped water from the underground Navajo Aquifer in a slurry pipeline operation to transport extracted coal to the Mohave Generating Station in Laughlin, Nevada. The Navajo Aquifer (N-aquifer) is the main source of potable water for the Navajo and Hopi tribes, who use the water for farming and livestock maintenance as well as drinking and other domestic uses. The tribes have alleged that the pumping of water by Peabody Energy has caused a severe decline in potable water and contamination of water sources. Both tribes, situated in an arid semi-desert, attach religious significance to water, considering it sacred, and have cultural, religious, and practical objections to over-use of water.

The Peabody mine, a coal strip mine, used the slurry to pump its coal through pipes 273 miles away where the coal could be filtered and used in the Mohave Generating Station in Laughlin, Nevada. The generating station produces energy for the southern parts of California and Nevada. This was the only coal slurry operation in the country and only plant that used groundwater in such a way.

The Black Mesa Mine's last day of operation was December 31, 2005. One of the power plants served by the coal mined at the location had the highest emission levels in the Western United States.

The Office of Surface Mining approved Peabody's permit request to continue operations at the mine on 22 December, 2008

Hopi mythology:

The **Hopi** maintain a complex religious and mythological tradition stretching back over centuries. However, it is difficult to definitively state what all Hopis as a group believe. Like the oral traditions of many other societies, Hopi mythology is not always told consistently and each Hopi mesa, or even each village, may have its own version of a particular story. But, "in essence the variants of the Hopi myth bear marked similarity to one another." It is also not clear that those stories which are told to non-Hopis, such as anthropologists and ethnographers, represent genuine Hopi beliefs or are merely stories told to the curious while keeping safe the Hopi's more sacred doctrines. As folklorist Harold Courlander states, "there is a Hopi reticence about discussing matters that could be considered ritual secrets or religion-oriented traditions." David Roberts continues that "the secrecy that lies at the heart of Puebloan [including Hopi] life . . . long predates European contact, forming an intrinsic feature of the culture." In addition, the Hopis have always been willing to assimilate foreign ideas into their cosmology if they are proven effective for such practical necessities as bringing rain. As such, the Hopi had at least some contact with Europeans beginning the 16th century, and some believe that European Christian traditions may have entered into Hopi cosmology at some point. Indeed, Spanish missions were built in several Hopi villages starting in 1629 and were in operation until the Pueblo Revolt of 1680. However, after the revolt, it was the Hopi alone of all the Pueblo tribes who kept the Spanish out of their villages permanently, and regular contact with whites did not begin again until nearly two centuries later. The Hopi mesas have therefore been seen as "relatively unacculturated" at least through the early twentieth century, and it may be posited that the European influence on the core themes of Hopi mythology was slight.

Major deities:

Most Hopi accounts of creation center around Tawa, the Sun Spirit. Tawa is the Creator, and it was he who formed the First World out of Tokpella, or Endless Space, as well as its original inhabitants. It is still traditional for Hopi mothers to seek a blessing from the Sun for their newborn children. However, other accounts have it that Tawa, or Taiowa, first created Sotuknang, whom he called his nephew. Taiowa then sent Sotuknang to create the nine universes according to his plan, and it was Sotuknang who created Spider Woman, or Spider Grandmother. Spider Woman served as a messenger for the Creator and was an intercessorary between deity and the people. In some versions of the Hopi creation myth, it is she who creates all life under the direction of Sotuknang. Yet other stories tell that life was created by Hard Being Woman of the West and Hard Being Woman of the East, while the Sun merely observed the process.

Masauwu, Skeleton Man, was the Spirit of Death and the Keeper of Fire. He was also the Master of the Upper World, or the Fourth World, and was there when the good people escaped the wickedness of the Third World for the promise of the Fourth. Masauwu is described as wearing a hideous mask, but again showing the diversity of myths among the Hopi, Masauwu was alternately described as a handsome, bejeweled man beneath his mask or as a bloody, fearsome creature. However, he is also assigned certain benevolent attributes. One story has it that it was Masauwu who helped settle the Hopi at Oraibi and gave them stewardship over the land. He also charged them to watch for the coming of the Pahana (see section below), the Lost White Brother. Other important deities include the twin war gods, the kachinas, and the trickster Coyote.

Maize is also vital to Hopi subsistence and religion. "For traditional Hopis, corn is the central bond. Its essence, physically, spiritually, and symbolically, pervades their existence. For the people of the mesas corn is sustenance, ceremonial object, prayer offering, symbol, and sentient being unto itself. Corn is the Mother in the truest sense that people take in the corn and the corn becomes their flesh, as mother milk becomes the flesh of the child."

Feminist interpretations:

Some contemporary writers tend to posit an absolute importance of the feminine to the Hopi and attribute the role of a male Creator (Tawa) to intrusions into Hopi folklore of European beliefs. In this interpretation, the Hopis traditionally saw the goddess Spider Woman as their creator, "Grandmother of the sun and as the great Medicine Power who sang the people into this fourth world we live in now." The theory holds that under centuries of pressure by white culture, Spider Woman has only recently been replaced by a male Creator and "the Hopi goddess Spider Woman has become the masculine Maseo or Tawa . . ."

While this view of Hopi mythology is deeply controversial, certainly the Hopi have much in their culture and mythology which emphasized the importance of the feminine. For instance, the Hopi are a matrilineal society, and children belong to the clan of the mother, not the father. The Hopi Mother Nature is symbolized by both Mother Earth and the Corn Mother. "Spider Woman, Sand Altar Woman, and other female spirits [are] conceived to be the mothers of all living things. This mother is represented in the cult by the sipapu, the opening in the floor of the underground ceremonial chamber, or kiva, for the sipapu is the womb of Mother Earth, just as it is the hole through which humankind originally emerged from the underworld."

However, Hopi religion was and is presided over by men, as were most political functions within the villages. Most importantly, it was only men who perform the required dances and ceremonies which brought rain to the Hopi.

Four Worlds:

Hopi legend tells that the current earth is the Fourth World to be inhabited by Tawa's creations. The story essentially states that in each previous world, the people, though originally happy, became disobedient and lived contrary to Tawa's plan; they engaged in sexual promiscuity, fought one another and would not live in harmony. Thus, the most obedient were led (usually by Spider Woman) to the next higher world, with physical changes occurring both in the people in the course of their journey, and in the environment of the next world. In some stories, these former worlds were then destroyed along with their wicked inhabitants, whereas in others the good people were simply led away from the chaos which had been created by their actions.

Entrance into the Fourth World:

Two main versions exist as to the Hopi's emergence into the present Fourth World. The more prevalent is that Spider Grandmother caused a hollow reed (or bamboo) to grow into the sky, and it emerged in the Fourth World at the *sipapu*. The people then climbed up the reed into this world, emerging from the *sipapu*. The location of the *sipapu* is given as in the Grand Canyon.

The other version (mainly told in Oraibi) has it Tawa destroyed the Third World in a great flood. Before the destruction, Spider Grandmother sealed the more righteous people into hollow reeds which were used as boats. Upon arriving on a small piece of dry land, the people saw nothing around them but more water, even after planting a large bamboo shoot, climbing to the top, and looking about. Spider Woman then told the people to make boats out of more reeds, and using island "stepping-stones" along the way, the people sailed east until they eventually arrived on the mountainous coasts of the Fourth World.

While it may not be possible to positively ascertain which is the original or "more correct" story, Harold Courlander writes, at least in Oraibi (the oldest of the Hopi villages), little children are often told the story of the *sipapu*, and the story of an ocean voyage is related to them when they are older. He states that even the name of the Hopi Water Clan (Patkinyamu) literally means "A Dwelling-on-Water" or "Houseboat". However, he notes the *sipapu* story is centered around Walpi and is more accepted among Hopis generally. Frank Waters is somewhat more insistent, and asserts the entire story of the *sipapu*, especially its proferred location in the Grand Canyon, merely symbolizes the Hopi tale of a water voyage from the West. In this interpretation, the Colorado River represents the western ocean while the cliffs of the canyon represent the Fourth World's rocky coasts.

Migrations:

Upon their arrival in the Fourth World, the Hopis divided and went on a series of great migrations throughout the land. Sometimes they would stop and build a town, then abandon it to continue on with the migration. However, they would leave their symbols behind in the rocks to show that the Hopi had been there. Long the divided people wandered in groups of families, eventually forming clans named after an event or sign that a particular group received upon its journey. These clans would travel for some time as a unified community, but almost inevitably a disagreement would occur, the clan would split and each portion would go its separate way. However, as the clans traveled, they would often join together forming large groups, only to have these associations disband, and then be reformed with other clans. These alternate periods of harmonious living followed by wickedness, contention, and separation play an important part of the Hopi mythos. This pattern seemingly began in the First World and continues even into recent history.

In the course of their migration, each Hopi clan was to go to the farthest extremity of the land in every direction. Far in the north was a land of snow and ice which was called the Back Door, but this was closed to the Hopi. However, the Hopi say that other peoples came through the Back Door into the Fourth World. This Back Door could be referring to the Bering land bridge, which connected Asia with far north North America. The Hopi clans also passed through the tropics in the south, and today many Hopis regard the Aztecs, Mayas, and other Central and South American Indian groups as renegade Hopi clans that never finished their appointed migrations. The Hopi were led on their migrations by various signs, or were helped along by Spider Woman. Eventually, the Hopi clans finished their prescribed migrations and were led to their current location in northeastern Arizona.

Jacob Hamblin, a Mormon missionary who first visited the Hopi in 1858, records a tradition that the Hopis were brought to their mesas by three prophets, and were not to cross the Colorado River to the west until these prophets had returned again. The idea that the Hopi were not to cross the Colorado or Rio Grande Rivers without permission is echoed in Frank Waters' work, although without mention of "three prophets." Waters continues that the Hopi settled in their desert land at the behest of Masauwu so that "they would have to depend upon the scanty rainfall which they must evoke with their power and prayer, and so preserve always that knowledge and faith in the supremacy of their Creator who had brought them to this Fourth World after they had failed in three previous worlds." In any case, most Hopi traditions have it that they were given their land by Masauwu, the Spirit of Death and Master of the Fourth World.

The Sacred Hopi Stones:

Hopi tradition tells of sacred tablets which were imparted to the Hopi by various deities. Like most of Hopi mythology, accounts differ as to when the tablets were given and in precisely what manner.

Perhaps the most important was said to be in the possession of the Fire Clan, and is related to the return of the Pahana. In one version, an elder of the Fire Clan worried that his people would not recognize the Pahana when he returned from the east. He therefore etched various designs including a human figure into a stone, and then broke off the section of the stone which included the figure's head. This section was given to Pahana and he was told to bring it back with him so that the Hopi would not be deceived by a witch or sorcerer.

Another version has it that the Fire Clan was given a sacred tablet by Masauwu, who as the giver of fire was their chief deity. In this version the human figure was purposely drawn without a head, and a corner of the stone was broken off. Masauwu told them that eventually the Pahana would return bringing the broken-off corner of the stone, but if in the meantime a Hopi leader accepted a false religion, he must assent to having his head cut off as drawn on the stone.

This same story holds that three other sacred tablets were also given to the Hopi. These were given to the Bear Clan by their patron deity Söqömhonaw, and essentially constituted a divine title to the lands where the Hopi settled after their migrations. The Hopi had a Universal Snake Dance. The third of these was etched with designs including the sun, moon, stars, clouds, etc. on one side with six human figures on the other.

Author Frank Waters claims that he was shown this third tablet in Oraibi in 1960. He describes the stone as "approximately 10 inches long, 8 inches wide, and 1 1/2 inches thick. The stone resembled a dull gray marble with intrusive blotches of rose." The physical existence of such a stone is substantiated by a few other sources. For instance, in the late 19th century, several Mormon missionaries were visiting a Hopi named Tuba in Oraibi. Tuba took his visitors inside the village kiva and once there, he produced what appeared to be a marble slab about 15"x18". This was covered in "hieroglyphic" markings including clouds and stars. As well, the later Ethnological Report No. 4 produced by the US government seems to uphold the existence of such a stone, based on the testimony of John W. Young and Andrew S. Gibbons. This describes the stone as made of "red-clouded marble, entirely different from anything found in the region."

Waters writes that these tablets again rose to great importance around the turn of the twentieth century as a result of trouble at Oraibi. This trouble involved a split between those called the Friendlies, who supported the efforts of the US government, and the Hostiles who opposed these efforts. The split was further exacerbated by old clan rivalries. The Bear Clan led the Friendly faction, and was strenuously opposed by the Spider and the Fire Clans, which led the Hostile faction. Finally, in 1906, there was a "push war" at Oraibi wherein the Friendlies pushed the Hostiles over a line which had been drawn on the ground. The Hostiles were thereafter banished from Oraibi and created the village of Hotevilla. The tablets were seen as important in that the Bear Clan tablets determined the traditional settlement pattern of the clans and the boundaries of Hopi lands as well as investing the clan with symbolic authority. However, the Fire Clan tablet was intimately connected with the return of Pahana and gave the Fire Clan claim to great importance. The tablets were also studied as prophetic and were believed to hold answers for the Hopi in the midst of their great dilemma. Waters claims that during the infighting, one of the Bear Clan tablets were stolen by another clan, and that for the time being all have been hidden. However, he maintains that they still exist, as evidenced by the tablet which he was shown in 1960. A letter from the Hopi to the President of the United States in 1949 also declared that "the Stone Tablets, upon which are written the boundaries of the Hopi Empire, are still in the hands of the Chiefs of Oraibi and Hotevilla pueblos . . ."

Kachinas:

Historically speaking, the kachina cult long predates European contact, and traces of the religion have been found which date to as early as 1325 A.D. However, it remains an open question among scholars as to whether the kachina religion was an indigenous creation, or an import from Mexico. The similarity of many aspects of Hopi religion to that of the Aztecs to the south strongly suggest the latter to many scholars. For example, the Hopi horned or plumed serpent Awanyu uncannily resembles the Aztec Quetzecoatl, as does the Hopi legend of the Pahana.</ref>

To the Hopi, kachinas are supernatural beings who represent and have charge over various aspects of the natural world. They might be thought of as analogous to Greco-Roman demi-gods or Catholic saints. There are literally hundreds of different Kachinas, which may represent anything from rain to watermelon, various animals, stars, and even other Indian tribes. However, the kachinas are also thought to be the spirits of dead ancestors, and they may come to the Hopi mesas in the form of rain clouds.

The Hopi say that during a great drought, they heard singing and dancing coming from the San Francisco Peaks. Upon investigation, they met the Kachinas who returned with the Hopi to their villages and taught them various forms of agriculture. The Hopi believe that for six months out of the year, the Kachina spirits live in the Hopi villages. After the Home

Dance in late July or early August, the Kachinas return to the San Francisco Peaks for six months. The Hopi believe that these dances are vital for the continued harmony and balance of the world. It serves the further and vital purpose of bringing rain to the Hopi's parched homeland.

Pahana:

> The true Pahana (*or* Bahana) is the "Lost *White* Brother" of the Hopi. Most versions have it that the Pahana or Elder Brother left for the east at the time that the Hopi entered the Fourth World and began their migrations. However, the Hopi say that he will return again and at his coming the wicked will be destroyed and a new age of peace, the Fifth World, will be ushered into the world. As mentioned above, it is said he will bring with him a missing section of a sacred Hopi stone in the possession of the Fire Clan, and that he will come wearing red. Traditionally, Hopis are buried facing *eastward* in expectation of the Pahana who will come from that direction.
>
> The legend of the Pahana seems *intimately* connected with the Aztec story of Quetzalcoatl, and other legends of Central America. This similarity is furthered by the liberal representation of Awanyu, the horned or *plumed serpent*, in Hopi and other Puebloan art. This figure bears a striking resemblance to figures of Quetzacoatl, the feathered serpent, in Mexico. In the early 16th century, both the Hopis and the Aztecs believed that the coming of the Spanish conquistadors was the return of this *lost white* prophet. Unlike the Aztecs, upon first contact the Hopi put the Spanish through a series of tests in order to determine their divinity, and having failed, the Spanish were sent away from the Hopi mesas.
>
> One account has it that the Hopi realized that the Spanish *were not* the Pahana based upon the destruction of a Hopi town by the Spanish. Thus when the Spanish arrived at the village of Awatovi, they drew a line of cornmeal as a sign for the Spanish not to enter the village, but this was ignored. While some Hopi wanted to fight the invaders, it was decided to try a peaceful approach in the hope that the Spanish would eventually leave. However, Spanish accounts record a short skirmish at Awatovi before the Hopis capitulated. Frank Waters records a Hopi tradition that the Spanish did ignore a cornmeal line drawn by the Hopis and a short battle followed.
>
> Tovar [the leader of the Spanish] and his men were conducted to Oraibi. They were met by all the clan chiefs at Tawtoma, as prescribed by prophecy, where four lines of sacred meal were drawn. The Bear Clan

leader stepped up to the barrier and extended his hand, palm up, to the leader of the white men. If he was indeed the true Pahana, the Hopis knew he would extend his own hand, palm down, and clasp the Bear Clan leader's hand to form the nakwach, the ancient symbol of brotherhood. Tovar instead curtly commanded one of his men to drop a gift into the Bear chief's hand, believing that the Indian wanted a present of some kind. Instantly all the Hopi chiefs knew that Pahana had forgotten the ancient agreement made between their peoples at the time of their separation. Nevertheless, the Spaniards were escorted up to Oraibi, fed and quartered, and the agreement explained to them. It was understood that when the two were finally reconciled, each would correct the other's laws and faults; they would live side by side and share in common all the riches of the land and join their faiths in one religion that would establish the truth of life in a spirit of universal brotherhood. The Spaniards did not understand, and having found no gold, they soon departed.

Texas:

Ysleta del Sur Pueblo, El Paso, Texas (Ysleta, Texas has been annexed into El Paso),—Tigua (Tiwa) speakers. Also spelled 'Isleta del Sur Pueblo'. This Pueblo was established in 1680 as a result of the Pueblo Revolt. Some 400 members of Isleta, Socorro and neighboring Pueblos were forced or accompanied the Spaniards to El Paso as they fled Northern New Mexico. Three missions (Ysleta, Socorro, and San Elizario) were established on the Camino Real to Santa Fe. Some of the Piru Puebloans settled in Senecu, and then in Socorro, Texas, adjacent to Ysleta, Texas (which is now within El Paso city limits). When the Rio Grande would flood the valley or change course, these missions would lie variously on the north or south sides of the river.

Colorado:

For most of the 12th and 13th centuries, known archaeologically as the Classic Period, the Ancient Puebloan Indians lived in the cliff dwellings at Mesa Verde. The reason for their sudden departure about 1275 remains unexplained. The San Ildefonso Pueblo claim their ancestors dwelled at Mesa Verde.

Feast days

January:
>Pojoaque Pueblo Feast Day: December 12, January 6
>San Ildefonso Pueblo Feast Day: January 23.

May:
>San Felipe Pueblo Feast Day: May 1

June:
>Ohkay Owingeh Pueblo Feast Day: June 24
>Sandia Pueblo Feast Day: June 13.
>Ysleta / Isleta del Sur Pueblo Feast Day: June 13.

July:
>Cochiti Pueblo Feast Day: July 14
>Santa Ana Pueblo Feast Day: July 26

August:
>Picuris Pueblo Feast Day: August 10
>Jemez Pueblo Feast Day: August 2
>Santo Domingo Pueblo Feast Day: August 4
>Zia Pueblo Feast Day: August 15

September:
>Acoma Pueblo Feast Day of San Esteban del Rey: September 2
>Laguna Pueblo Feast Day: September 19
>Taos Pueblo Feast Day: September 30

October:
>Nambe Pueblo Feast Day of St. Francis: October 4

December:
>Pojoaque Pueblo Feast Day: December 12, January 6
>Variable
>Isleta Pueblo Feast Days

Pottery:

There is a long history of creating pottery among the various Pueblo communities. Mera, in his discussion of the "Rain Bird" motif, a common and popular design element in pueblo pottery states that, "In tracing the ancestry of the "Rain Bird" design it will be necessary to go back to the very beginnings of decorated pottery in the Southwest to a ceramic type which as reckoned by present day archaeologists came into existence some time during the early centuries of the Christian era."

Well-known Puebloan potters include Maria Montoya Martinez.

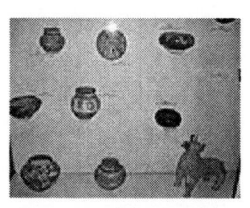

Pottery of the Pueblo people, Field Museum, Chicago

Zia Pueblo, pottery bowl, Field Museum

Tesuque Pueblo Pottery Jar, Field Museum

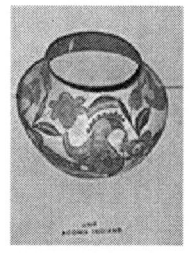

Acoma Pueblo, pottery jar, Field Museum

Tesuque Pueblo, Pottery Jar, Field Museum

San Ildefonso Pueblo, Black-on-Black Pottery Bowl. Field Museum

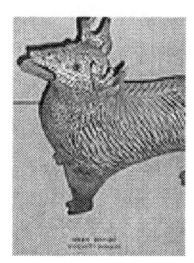

Deer effigy, pottery. Cicuye Pueblo, Field Museum

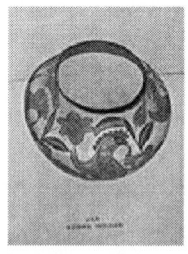

Pottery Jar, Acoma Pueblo, taken at Field Museum

Pottery Canteen, Acoma Pueblo, taken at Field Museum

Attachment:

The kachinas, an alien intelligence, but not as we know it
For centuries, the Hopi of Arizona have been intimately liaising with beings from the Otherworld. The kachinas still visit the Hopi Mesas on an annual basis and their presence continues to set out the agenda of Hopi society.

Philip Coppens

In July 1947, an alien craft allegedly crash-landed in Roswell, New Mexico. If it occurred, it was not the first of its kind: the region of New Mexico and Arizona has a history of "alien contacts" that goes back hundreds if not thousands of years. The beings in questions are known as "kachinas"; they are not extra-terrestrial as such, but definitely otherworldly.

An extensive collection of 400 kachina dolls can be seen in the Heard Museum in Phoenix; they were donated by the controversial Republican politician Barry Goldwater. Each doll looks different and has specific characteristics; each represents a different element or entity that has entered the Hopi world at some point in their history. And when you look at the Eototo kachina doll in the Museum of Northern Arizona, you find the creature has much in common with LEGO figures. Then again, just like LEGO, kachina dolls were there for children be educated in the ways of the Otherworld and how it interacted with ours.

Amongst the Native Americans, the Hopi have a special place. Thousands of people would like to visit their religious ceremonies, and thousands of tourists return home from Arizona with a kachina doll.

The kachina dolls are made from kaolin clay, meant to be hung from beams or walls in the home. They are white in colour and the basic shape is painted to show a head, arms, folded over a kilt, which is representing rain. Tradition argues that carving the "tihu" should be done by men, but today, women are involved in their manufacture, if only for selling them to tourists. Indeed, in what is likely to be a rush for finance, rather than heritage, tribal councils even tried to copyright the word kachina, but failed to do so.

Though the kachina dolls are often identified with the Hopi deities, this is highly inaccurate: one should not confuse the dolls with the kachina themselves. The dolls are merely props and many have fallen for the mistake, to take the prop for the god.

One might argue that their closest parallel is the voodoo doll or the Egyptian ushabti—though one needs to de-cinematise these artefacts in order to appreciate their true role and function. Indeed, one of the reasons that many of the ceremonies of the Hopi are now closed to outsiders is because a Marvel comic had characterized the kachina as violent avengers.

The kachina themselves—rather than the dolls—are largely described as "spirit messengers", whereas some believe they might represent the spirit of the dead—if there were a difference. The Hopi state that at one time in the past, the kachina deities visited the Mesas in person, but that they now do so in the form of masked dancers.

Whereas kachina dolls are sold and hung from beams or walls, the real deities are surrounded with far greater respect. The Hopi deities live on the San Francisco Mountains, though are present amongst the Hopi for part of the year. As such, the religious year is divided into two parts.

The deities arrive at the Hopi Mesas in the form of rain-bearing clouds and normally arrive in early February for the Powamuya ceremony, or Bean Dance. The Hopi do indeed believe that in the past, the deities literally walked amongst them, but that today, their presence resides in those selected to wear a mask; it is the mask that transforms the Hopi individual into a "possessed" entity, very much like Jim Carrey in the movie "The Mask"—though it is clear that, just like with the voodoo dolls, the evil and negative connotations that have been introduced in these movies are for entertainment value only.

Three main ceremonies are performed by and for the gods—katsinam—during their stay in the villages: Soyalangwu, a winter solstice ceremony held in December; the already mentioned Powamuya in February, when the katsinam are asked to appear; and Niman, the home-going ceremony, after the summer solstice. Between Powamuya and Niman, the Hopi perform several more dances in honour of the deities. Early in the year they are held in underground ceremonial chambers called kivas, but as spring arrives, the dances move out onto the plazas, where they last from morning until dusk.

The fraternities in charge of the summer dances meet in mid-winter for ceremonial smoking and the planting of prayer plumes. In late November, a chief kachina, Soyalkatsina, begins the kachina season by walking along the trail into the village like a weary old man or someone who has had too much sleep, singing sacred songs in a low voice. He then opens the main kiva, signalling that it is time for the katsinam to come out. Their emergence re-enacts the arrival of the Hopi into the present, Fourth World.

Each December, a runner climbs to a shrine in the San Francisco Peaks, where he scatters a meal and plants plumes that are to be brought back in July, by another runner, for the final festival, Niman, linked with the harvest. At the harvest festival, the deities return to the underworld, through the San Francisco Peaks. Interestingly, it is claimed that the seasons in the Underworld are one season behind.

As mentioned, the actual return of the deities to the Hopi Mesas is celebrated at Powamu, the Bean-Planting Ceremony in February. Each matriarch receives a bundle of fresh bean sprouts to plant for the coming year. The festival lasts eight days and concludes with dancing, which takes place in the nine kivas of the mesa. Everyone wears fresh mud from the sacred spring and each job of plastering has been signed with the print of the slim hand of the girl who did it.

All Hopi babies receive a tihu—a kachina doll—at their first Niman ceremony, while the girls receive further dolls at each Powamuya and Niman ceremony, up until or near marriageable age, although married women sometimes still get them from their husbands. The dolls are created as a teaching tool given to these children and is presented to them by one of the masked dancers. Boys and girls are normally properly initiated into society between the age of six to ten, when they are allowed to participate in the performances and discover that the masked dancers are their own relatives—very much like finding out who Santa Claus really is—though I, of course, never said that.

There is a clear relationship between the deities and the kachina dolls, the latter representing aspects of the former. Hopi katsinam can be male or female, and represent plants, animals, insects, human qualities, the creative force of the sun, and even death. Some are demons who frighten children into behaving properly; most are clan ancestors and beneficent beings. They are messengers who accept Hopi gifts and prayers for health, fertility, and rain and carry them back to the gods. Their role as rainmakers is particularly important to the Hopi. The deities are present, either in the statues, or the sacred masks. Unlike the dolls, the masks are sacred objects and the Hopi have successfully petitioned to remove them from museum displays.

The katsinam is and can therefore be a spirit of any kind—very much on par with the ever growing list of Catholic saints that can be implored. The masks could be compared to the Christian holy relics. But just like Roman Catholic statues, no sacred power is invested in the kachina doll. Unlike Roman Catholic statues, the kachina dolls are not used in ceremonies, nor are they preserved in the kiva. They are simply . . . dolls, so that children play with them and learn how to interact with the various spirits and otherworldly entities that are part of the tribe's daily life.

There are nevertheless sacred statues preserved in the kiva, known as wu'ya or tiponi. The wu'ya is a clan deity, and a tiponi is a fetish of stone or wood, representing the deity. Unlike the kachina dolls, these are seldom brought out in to the open, their use normally reserved for ritual use inside the kiva.

Indeed, in 1960, the so-called "Vernon man" was discovered. Nine inches high, carved from sandstone and painted with vertical stripes, this statue was found in a crypt within a kiva. Though popularly also labelled a kachina, the Hopi identify it as a wu'ya or tiponi, a clan deity.

The kachina doll cult is known to have definitely existed by 1300 AD. Some argue it came from the Zuni Pueblo to the West of the Hopi Mesas, others argue that it came from the Rio Grande, others that it came from the Members cult of the south, and/or that it developed in Mexico. In short: no-one knows. Details of the paintings on Awatovi murals, an ancestral Hopi site, show costumed and masked figures as separated elements or interacting in scenes. But the role and iconography of the dolls does strongly echo certain Aztec deities such as Tlaloc, the god of rain, and Quetzalcoatl, the feathered serpent, who was also the bringer of rain and corn. Seeing the kachina are specifically linked with the rain . . .

Recent discoveries in Chaco Canyon have also suggested that the kachina cult was introduced by cannibalistic warrior refugees from the south. It is clear that this archaeological discovery—or at least the conclusion drawn from it—has created controversy within the Native American community.

Wherever it came from, representations of masked beings that have the characteristics of the kachina appear on murals in kivas that date to as early as 1350. Situated at Hopi and Homol'ovi on the Hopi Mesas themselves, it underlines the length of time in which the cult has been present amongst the Hopi people.

Though all deities are equal, some are more popular than others, the most famous for outside is Kokopelli, a fertility deity, usually depicted as a humpbacked flute player (often with a huge phallus and feathers or antenna-like protrusions on his head). Like most fertility deities, Kokopelli presides over both childbirth and agriculture, but he is also a trickster god and represents the spirit of music.

Interestingly, Kokopelli is one of the most easily recognized figures found in the petroglyphs and pictographs of the Southwest, the earliest known petroglyph depicting him dating to about 1000 AD. It underlines that there is—at least in the case of some deities—a tradition that has spanned a millennium.

Just how old the cult truly is, no-one knows. In the dances, the Kokopilua kachina dancer sings a song in a language so ancient that not a word of it is understood by the modern Hopi themselves, who know only that their deities have accompanied them throughout their migrations . . . and continue to visit them annually at the Mesas.

Outsiders want to experience the Hopi ceremonies, but are unlikely to truly capture the essence of the activities. A Hopi Indian has been raised, from birth, in a tradition, surrounded by dolls that represented otherworldly creatures that are nevertheless part of their world and daily life. These entities did not crash-land just one day somewhere; these entities have been with them for thousands of years, and continue to interact with the Hopi in a manner that only a Hopi can truly understand.

This article appeared in FENIX Magazine Issue 17.

Acknowledgement

All of the material in this book are taken-from the Internet free encyclopaedia "Wikipedia".

CPSIA information can be obtained at www.ICGtesting.com
Printed in the USA
269149BV00001B/77/P